LAWNS

AND GROUND COVERS

W9-CZF-906

A Sunset Book

LAWNS
AND GROUND COVERS

BY THE SUNSET EDITORIAL STAFF
under the direction of Joseph F. Williamson
Garden Editor, Sunset Magazine

LANE BOOKS • MENLO PARK, CALIFORNIA

Acknowledgments

We would like to acknowledge the assistance of the following lawn and ground cover experts in the preparation of this book: David E. Bayer, Extension Weed Control Specialist, University of California, Davis; Roy L. Branson, Extension Soils and Water Specialist, University of California, Riverside; the late Mrs. Helen Buzard, Garden Consultant, Bellevue, Washington; Robert D. Danielson, Asst. Professor of Landscape Horticulture, University of California, Davis; Clarence E. Godshalk, Director, The Morton Arboretum, Lisle, Illinois; Roy L. Goss, Turf Agronomist, Western Washington Experiment Station, Puyallap; C. J. Gould, Plant Pathologist, Western Washington Experiment Station, Puyallup; William Harvey, Extension Weed Control Specialist, University of California, Davis; Angus J. Howitt, Associate Entomologist, Western Washington Experiment Station, Puyallup; Eric Johnson, Landscape Designer, Monrovia, California; John H. Madison, Jr., Asst. Professor of Landscape Horticulture, University of California, Davis; Armand M. Sarinana, Turf Management Specialist, San Gabriel, California; Robert W. Schery, Director, The Lawn Institute, Marysville, Ohio; H. L. Schudel, Turf Grass and Chemical Specialist, Corvallis, Oregon; Victor B. Youngner, Asst. Professor of Floriculture and Ornamental Horticulture, University of California, Los Angeles.

Executive Editor, Sunset Books: David E. Clark
Nineteenth Printing March 1975

*All rights reserved throughout the world. Third Edition. Copyright ©
1964 by Lane Magazine & Book Company, Menlo Park, California.
No part of this publication may be reproduced by any mechanical,
photographic, or electronic-process, or in the form of a phonographic
recording, nor may it be stored in a retrieval system, transmitted, or
otherwise copied for public or private use without prior witten
permission from the publisher. Library of Congress No. 64-15527.
SBN Title No. 350. Lithographed in the U.S.A.*

Table of Contents

Why Have a Lawn?

Come what may in new paving materials, in new low-maintenance landscaping schemes, in things we haven't even seen yet, and in new and bigger demands on hours that would otherwise go into lawn mowing—come all these things, nothing will ever take the place of a parcel of green, mowed turf.

• Nothing else feels so good to your bare feet.

• Nothing else will ever be as good for turning somersaults on, playing catch on, wrestling on, or serve so well as courts for games such as badminton and croquet.

• Nothing else does a better job of covering the soil in a garden while still allowing water and oxygen to reach tree and shrub roots in the soil below.

• Nothing else that is soft, spongy, and resilient can be raked and swept as easily.

• No paving material challenges and rewards the farmer instinct in us to the same degree.

The *Sunset* lawn book has existed since 1955, but it has undergone many revisions, necessitated by changes in the turfgrass business.

The latest set of changes, made for the eighth printing (September 1969), was brought about by a new awareness of the effects of certain insecticides. Previous editions of this book suggested using the insecticides aldrin, chlordane, DDT, dieldrin, and lindane. These insecticides break down very slowly and retain their chemical potency, wherever nature may take them, for years. And nature takes them all over the world. Presence of the insecticide in the world's sea water and other places indirectly causes reproductive failure—and possible extinction—of several bird species. *Sunset* no longer recommends these chemicals. This book gives substitute chemicals that are effective, do break down, do not persist, and do not indirectly damage the environment.

As you read through this book—especially the maintenance chapters—you will find that today's chemicals and equipment make lawn upkeep surprisingly simple.

When you see grass beginning to turn yellowish, the chances are that an application of almost any lawn fertilizer will get it growing fast and green again. In the arid parts of the West, watering is a mechanical habit, but should you slip up and forget, it will be both amazing and pleasing to see how quickly a good watering will make the grass perky again.

Mowing a lawn may take time (it doesn't take much muscle with today's mowers), but look what it does for the appearance of a lawn. Wouldn't it be nice if you could make an old carpet, or a rangy ivy bed, or even a concrete patio look as trim and neat again so easily?

Pulling weeds on hands and knees is hardly necessary at all any more. Selective chemicals can kill crabgrass several different ways, others can kill broad-leafed weeds like dandelions in just a few days, and now there are even selective killers for the previously impossible weeds, like yellow oxalis, in dichondra lawns.

There is one final point we'd like to emphasize. We have looked at enough home lawns (thousands of them) and enough demonstration turf plots (hundreds of them) to be positive that no two lawns anywhere are alike, and never will be. So many things vary—the soils, the climates, the kinds of turf plants that grow in a lawn, the care they get, the way they were planted, the season of the year, even how high the sun is in the sky at the moment you look at the grass. You can see why your lawn has to be different in some degree from your neighbor's, or from a lawn in the next town or the next state.

In this book you will find straight, definite directions for some parts of lawn planting and lawn care. But in other places you will find recommendations hanging from a series of "ifs" and "howevers," particularly when it comes to diagnosing ills. We think that you won't mind the qualifications so much, and in time will even come to appreciate them, because they show you the considerations that a lawn expert would have to reckon with if he were managing your lawn. When you can diagnose with all of the variables in mind, your real lawn problems will be at an end.

Your Choices in Lawn Grasses

There are about 1,500 different kinds of grasses growing in the United States. This figure includes pasture grasses, range grasses, and such wayward members of the grass family as bamboo, corn, and sugar cane. Only about forty types of grass have a place in lawns, but even this number gives you a multitude of choices.

In addition, there are a few broad-leafed plants (not grasses) that grow low, flat, and green, and therefore are lawn plants: dichondra, now widely used in California and Arizona (see page 76); and lippia, Irish moss, and a few other walk-on ground covers (described in the ground cover chapter).

However, the forty or so grasses make almost all of the lawns in the country. Grasses have these anatomical points in common:

Leaves grow alternately in two rows up the side of the jointed stems. The space between the joints may be hollow or pithy. A sheath surrounds the stem above each joint. Follow the sheath up the stem, and you come to a collar-like growth (called the auricle) which clasps the stem at the top of the sheath. The blade grows outward, and usually upward, from this collar. The particular arrangement of sheath, auricle, ligule, and blade helps botanists and grass seed growers to identify many of the common lawn grasses in the absence of flower or seed-spike which is the true botanical identifier. Other aids to identification: shape of leaves, thickness of stem, means of spreading—stolons or underground stems known as rhizomes—and color.

Grass blades elongate from the lower end, so that when you mow off the tips, the leaves renew their length from the other end or new leaves come up from the base. This characteristic is what makes grasses unique and universally adapted to use for close-cropped ground cover.

There are two lawn variety charts on the following pages—one for cool-season grasses and one for warm-

COOL-SEASON GRASSES

SUBTROPICAL GRASSES

SUNSET LAWN. This is part of the 3½-acre Sunset lawn in Menlo Park, California, originally a mixture of 20 per cent creeping red fescue, 10 per cent Merion blue, 10 per cent Astoria bent, 60 per cent Kentucky blue. Lawn is fertilized monthly. Header board around tree bed set flush with lawn so mower can pass over it

season subtropical grasses. Each class has its own part of the country. A line could be drawn all the way across the United States that would separate the two regions. North of the line is cool-season grass country. South of the line is subtropical grass and dichondra country. Of course, any such line is subject to argument, especially right along the border. But if you go very far north of the line it is impossible to grow the frost-tender subtropical grasses; in the borderline areas you may have only the cool-season grasses, but unless you strive mightily to keep them happy through the summer months, they will languish and the mighty and ever-present subtropical grasses (chiefly common Bermuda grass) will come and crowd them out.

Some people are willing to spend the time and money it takes to keep a cool-season grass in the subtropical grass country, probably because bluegrass is still looked upon by many people as the only real lawn grass. Generally, the most common use for the cool-season grasses in the heart of the subtropical grass country is to sow in fall as "winter grass" over the subtropical grass lawns. It hides the subtropical grasses' dormant brown color (page 75).

Evaluation of cool-season grasses
(See chart starting on page 11)

These are the hardy or cool-season grasses—the staple items for lawns north of the horticultural Mason-Dixon line and for special uses south of the line.

Your main use for this chart will probably be to get a general idea of the lawn texture, color, and maintenance that can be expected from any particular seed mixture you might look at on the nursery or garden supply store shelves. For example, if you find a big percentage (over 35%) of a coarse grass such as meadow fescue, you will know that it probably will be a coarse-looking lawn. A good fine grass mix would be high in Kentucky bluegrass and would contain no rye grass. If the ingredient list shows any percentage of bents, you can figure that it will be a high maintenance lawn — the chart tells you that bents are very susceptible to summer diseases and that they need low mowing. If you are planting a lawn in shade, look on the mix' lists of ingredients for the varieties indicated as growing in shade.

Some single grass varieties are packaged and sold by

BERMUDA. Photograph shows stolons above ground, pieces of rhizomes underground. Plants spread by stolons or rhizomes. Low mowing keeps Bermuda tidy

themselves. They perform well enough as turf grasses to stand alone; other varieties are not considered necessary to supplement them.

A lawn of a single grass type is valuable in that it will give you uniform growth and exactly what you are after —all fine texture, all toughness, or whatever it may be. Its weakness is that if an unfortunate condition should develop to which the one grass were susceptible, your lawn could be wiped out.

At the opposite extreme are the mixtures that include a dozen or so varieties. Safety in numbers is the idea here. Each grass has its season of top performance; theoretically, you get top performance all year. In choosing a mix, it is best to select one containing no more than 3 to 4 varieties; otherwise the lawn becomes too uneven in color, texture, etc. Eventually, the lawn's make-up may dwindle to just 2 or 3 varieties, but they will be the ones that take best to your lawn's exposure, soil conditions, and to your watering habits, fertilizing program, and mowing height (if you have a bluegrass and bent mixture, you can kill the bluegrass out by mowing at ¾-inch height—only the bent would survive).

Never blame a lawn's failure on the seed—if you bought it from a reputable dealer. Good seed will germinate and come true; that's all you can expect from it. The rest of the grass' performance depends on its environment as you make it and keep it.

Prices favor buying fine-leafed, slow-growing mixes, even though they sell for more per pound. There are thousands more seeds per pound in most fine-leafed grasses than there are in the coarse ones. The fast-growing grasses generally have bigger seeds. Compare a typical

fine-leafed mix at $1.50 per pound to a hard-usage, fast-growing mix at 75 cents per pound. A pound of the first mix will cover 300 square feet; a pound of the other, 100 square feet. Matching coverage, you find the fine-leafed mix giving you 100 square feet for 50 cents, the other for 75 cents.

Evaluation of subtropical grasses (See chart starting on page 13)

These are the subtropical grasses, also called stoloniferous grasses because some of them spread rampantly by means of above-ground runners (stolons) and are frequently planted as sections of these stolons. In logical opposition to the term "cool-season grasses" charted on previous pages, these could be called "warm-season grasses." In most of the milder latitudes of the United States, the grasses charted on these pages grow vigorously in the warm season and go dormant in the cool season. Meanwhile, in the same regions, the "cool-season grasses" do the opposite; however, their summer dormancy is not so pronounced as is the subtropical grasses' winter dormancy. Both the hybrid Bermudas and the zoysias maintain a thick carpet during the winter, which keeps mud from being tracked into the house.

Shopping for subtropical grasses is a totally different matter than shopping for cool-season grasses. Instead of buying seeds in a box, you usually buy in one of these ways: bagged green stolons which are kept fresh and planted while still green, as outlined on page 22; squares of sod, with the dirt washed off, that you tear into sprigs and plant; flats of grass from which you plant plugs (page 22); rolled-up sod (page 21) ready to install on a lawn bed that has been prepared more or less the same way as for seeding.

Several big turfgrass growers in the southern states and in the Pacific Southwest grow these grasses. Your nursery may sell some of the grasses, or your nurseryman can probably help you place an order with one of the growers.

Common Bermuda grass, U-3 Bermuda, and Zoysia japonica are the only subtropical grasses from which seed is grown, packaged, and sold. The U-3 Bermuda seed is not considered very reliable. It segregates into many different types, producing an uneven turf. Seed of Zoysia japonica is even less satisfactory and not generally offered.

All of the hybrid Bermuda grasses cover faster than the zoysias from root-runners. All of the zoysias and hybrid Bermudas can substantially crowd out broad-leafed weeds.

An Evaluation of Cool-Season Grasses

		What does it look like?	What are its good points?	What are its bad points?	What special seasonal changes?	How to plant: Seeds, stolons, or sprigs.	Does it grow in the shade?	Best with high or lower mowing?	Comments on the entire genus or class.
BENT	ASTORIA	Fine leaves. Makes a thick turf. In different lawns color varies from dull green to light green (not as blue-gray as the others).	Texture is exceptionally uniform. Spreads by rooting at joints.	Not very vigorous. Gets summer diseases worse than any other bent. Tends to mat or thatch. Doesn't blend well with other grasses. Becomes chlorotic faster than others.	Healthy, compact growth in winter. Summer susceptibility to diseases makes it weak at that time.	Seeds	In sun or part shade, but not deep shade.	Cut at ¾ inch.	Astoria and Highland are Colonial bents. More erect than creepers. Will withstand the most neglect of the bents, but still need work to look their best.
	HIGHLAND	Fine, upright leaves. A grayish-green compared to bluish-green of Seaside and apple-green of Astoria.	Hardier and tougher than Astoria and more disease-tolerant. High survival rate under drought conditions.	Tends to form tufts or bunches when in mixed turf. Forms false crowns which give good appearance on top, but with a lot of crown fluff underneath. Rides up on other grasses. Subject to insect attack in late summer.	Strong growth in winter—Sept. to June. May tend to stand still during hot weather while crabgrass thrives.	"	"	"	All bent grasses are requiring careful attention to mowing, fertilizing, watering, and disease control.
	PENNCROSS	Fine, flat, narrow leaves. Dense. Bluish-green. Produced by selecting superior strains of Seaside and using them as seed parents.	It looks like Seaside, but it is healthier, more disease-resistant.	A vigorous strain. Needs frequent attention to mowing, thatch removal, fertilizing.		Seeds. Use ½ rate for Seaside. Smaller seed, greater vigor.	"	Definitely best with low (½-inch) mow.	This is the creeping bent. Grown regularly from seed which produces plants of wide variability. The varieties below have been selected from Seaside because of superior color, disease resistance, vigor, or other characteristics.
	SEASIDE	Fine, flat, narrow leaves. Dense. Bluish-green.	Uniform texture when well cared for.	Runners on lawn surface are visible more than on Astoria bent, and many other kinds of grasses. Quite susceptible to summer diseases. Seed mix gives patches of pale and dark green.	Makes slow but healthy, compact growth in the cool months—Sept. to June.	Seeds	In part shade, but not deep shade.	Definitely best with low (½-inch) mow.	
	CONGRESSIONAL	Very fine texture, medium to dark green color.	This one is above average in disease resistance among bents. Superior uniform color and texture, too.	Needs more care (in thatch control and mowing) than seed-grown bents.		Sprigs or stolons.		Needs frequent, low (½-inch) mowings.	These premium-quality, high-maintenance bents are available for planting only as stolons (sprigs of surface runners) or as sod (not as seed).
	OLD ORCHARD	Fine texture. Medium green color.	Very vigorous grower. Uniform color and texture, above average disease resistance.	"		"	"	"	
FINE FESCUES	CREEPING RED	Fine texture. Forms a dense turf.	Fine texture and good color. Texture mixes with that of bluegrasses.	Somewhat variable in appearance. Not permanent in most areas. Susceptible to red-thread disease.	Grass turns a little darker in winter.	Seeds	Yes. One of the varieties to look for in mixes for shady places.	Cut at 1½-2 inches.	All of these fine, rolled leaves—like tiny soft needles. Along with Kentucky bluegrass, the fescues comprise the heaviest portion of most fine-leafed lawn mixtures. Fescues are supposedly less particular about soil conditions than either bluegrass or bent grass, blend well with bluegrass, should not be used alone because they get clumpy. Fescues are fairly drought-tolerant. These grasses best in cool areas.
	ILLAHEE	Very fine texture, bright green color.	Color blends with bents and bluegrasses better than creeping red. Beautiful color.	Susceptible to summer diseases.	"	"	Yes.	"	
	RAINIER	In suitable climate it looks dainty, soft, and deep green (deeper green than Chewings or Illahee). Coarser texture than Illahee.	Has tested best of the fine fescues in two University of California test plots.	More tolerant of disease than Illahee, but not a strong hot-summer performer.	Grass turns a little darker in winter.	Seeds	Yes. One of the varieties to look for in mixes.	Cut at 1½-2 inches.	
	CHEWINGS	Same as Rainier but a grayer green. Duller colored than bluegrass.	Does better than most grasses where moisture and food are limited.	Does not heal fast after injury. Yellows in winter cold. Tends to grow in clumps more than the three above.	Winter yellows.	"	Yes.	Cut at 1½-2 inches.	

Evaluation of cool-season grasses (continued)

		What does it look like?	What are its good points?	What are its bad points?	What special seasonal changes?	How to plant . . . seeds or sprigs?	Does it grow in shade?	Best with high or low mowing?	Comments on the entire genus or class.
BLUE GRASSES	KENTUCKY	Forms a dense sod, leaves are dark green, smooth, upright and soft.	Many good points. Probably the best all-around lawn grass in the cool-season grass country. Spreads by rhizomes.	Susceptible to a number of diseases.	Slows in summer, grows fastest in cool season, but turns dormant in mid-winter with sustained freezing.	Seeds	Not very well, except in hot summer areas.	Cut not lower than 1½ inches.	Kentucky Bluegrass is not a pure strain. A lawn of it contains many distinct types (distinct to a grass expert). Merion, Newport, Windsor, Delta, and Park are special selections from Kentucky Blue. A mixture of seed of Merion, Newport or C-1, and Windsor combines the good qualities of each.
	MERION KENTUCKY	More prostrate grower and denser than ordinary Kentucky bluegrass. Dark blue-green.	More drought-resistant than Kentucky Blue. More tolerant of several diseases than common bluegrass. Withstands closer mowing and hard use.	Susceptible to a rust disease that is hard to control (see disease chapter). Needs extra feeding. Slow to germinate.	"	"	Better than Kentucky Blue.	Can be cut at ¾ inch, but 1½ inches is better.	
	NEWPORT or C-1	About the same texture as Merion. Upright growth like common Kentucky.	Looks well with somewhat less fertilizer than Merion.	Susceptible to rust and several other diseases.	"	"	Not very well, except in hot, summer areas.	"	
	WINDSOR	Low-lying, dense, intense blue-green, tends to creep.	Above average in disease resistance. Vigorous. Good spreading properties. Drought resistant.	Too new to tell (1964).	"	"	"	"	
	DELTA	Very similar to common Kentucky bluegrass. Finer, stiffer, more erect, but not as dense.	Survives more drying and possibly more heat than others. Less disease than common.	May appear thin and lumpy.	"	"	"	"	
	PARK	Very similar to common Bluegrass, but high seedling vigor. A mixture of several selected varieties.	Big, heavy seed, giving fast start and seedling vigor. Forms dense sod.	Susceptible to crown rot in extreme summer heat and other diseases.	"	"	"	"	
	POA TRIVIALIS	A fine-textured grass with upright leaves and an apple-green color.	No other grass grows as well in wet, shady, spots.	In warm areas it will survive only with shade and abundant water. Won't stand heavy wear, forms mat.	Can suffer in summer like bents.		Only in shade.		
RYE GRASSES	PERENNIAL	Usually medium-coarse with waxy sheen on the rather sparsely set leaves.	In some cases it is the easiest grass to grow. Good in wide variety of climates.	Too rough and bunchy for a "perfect carpet." Hard to mow in late summer.	Gets hard to mow in summer.	Seeds	Fairly well.	1½ inches is usually best.	Bunch grasses, so can never make a really tight, self-knitting turf. Temporary ground cover in Southwest.
	ANNUAL	Coarser than perennial rye.	Grows fast, hence used for quick cover and for winter grass on Bermuda lawns.	Does not live through winters in northern areas or summers in southern areas. Usually contains some perennial rye which will survive in clumps where you don't want it.	Most of it dies out in one year's time.	Seeds	Not very well.	1½ inches usually best.	
REDTOP	REDTOP	Similar to Astoria bent, but coarser in texture. Varies from coarse weedy clumps in spring to fine bent-grass type in late summer. Produces rhizomes.	Quick growing. Will grow in wet or dry soils, shade, or sun. Good for over-seeding Bermuda. Gives way to bluegrass in time.	Tends to clump or bunch in old turf as it thins out. Susceptible to diseases. Some agronomists say it has no good points.		Seeds	Not very well, except in hot summer areas.	Cut ¾ to 1 inch high.	Used primarily as temporary "nurse" grass. Less aggressive than rye grass in most climates. Component of mix for neglected, uncared for area that needs cover.

Evaluation of cool-season grasses (continued)

		What does it look like?	What are its good points?	What are its bad points?	What special seasonal changes?	How to plant: Seeds, stolons, or sprigs?	Does it grow in shade?	Best with high or lower mowing?	Comments on the entire genus or class.
COARSE FESCUES	MEADOW	Medium-coarse. Soft, pliant, dark green.	Quick-growing, but fairly permanent and tough. Better than rye for quick cover. Will give way in time to bluegrass in most areas. Good survival under tough city conditions: smog, dirt, some shade, etc.	Not as wear-resistant, permanent, or drought-tolerant as the three 'below'. Coarse growth.	None	Seeds	Not very well.	1½ inches is usually best.	All of these very wide-bladed, clumping grasses are best for football fields and lawns that get very rough treatment. Must be seeded at 8-10 lbs./1.000 square feet for best results. Sow as pure stand. In mix, coarse fescues develop as large, coarse weeds in lawns. Sow at heavy rate and texture will be finer.
	ALTA OR KENTUCKY 31	Coarser than Meadow.	Very wear-resistant, drought-resistant and long-lived. Will grow well in poor or very heavy soils. Good year around. No particular pests. Resists Bermuda longer. Best cool-season grass for hot climates.	May tend to clump in time. Very coarse texture limits its use. Once established it is almost impossible to get rid of without hand weeding. If neglected, gets tough. Bare areas fill in slowly.	Heavy flush of spring growth may require twice a week mowing for 4-5 weeks.	Seed at extra heavy rates, 10 lbs. to 1,000 sq. ft. Seed is cheap.	Light shade only.	Cut ¾ to 2 inches. At ¾ inch susceptible to weed invasion. Best cut with rotary mower.	
	GOARS	An improved form of Alta.	"	"	"	"	"	"	
CLOVER	CLOVER	Dark green, soft and lush, three-part compound leaf.	Can be controlled to a degree by fertilizing. High phosphate fertilizers encourage clover. Nitrogen pushes grasses.	Forms patches. Stains clothing badly.	No significant changes during the growing season.	Seeds	Yes, but gets lanky in deep shade.	High mowing encourages it. Low mowing discourages.	Under good conditions it manufactures its own nitrogen so that a grass and clover lawn generally needs less feeding.

An Evaluation of Subtropical Grasses

		What does it look like?	What are its good points?	What are its bad points?	Winter color retention?	How to plant: Seeds, sprigs, or stolons?	Does it grow in shade?	Best with high or low mowing?	Comments on the entire genus or class.
ZOYSIA GRASSES	Z. JAPONICA	Rather-coarse, as tropical grasses go. Blades are almost as wide as those of Alta Fescue.	Disease-resistant, drought-tolerant. Requires less feeding. Amenable to "winter grass" planting.	Requires long time to develop solid cover (1 to 2 years). Poor winter color. Heavy thatch.	Goes out in fall before Z. Matrella.	Seeds and sprigs or stolons (seed variable).	Yes, in areas with warm summer nights.	Best about 1½ inches.	When zoysias first came on market they suffered from irresponsible advertising (no grass is perfect!). Zoysia is outstanding for its strong, dense turf, once established (no weeds, Bermuda, insects, or diseases). Its one big fault is dormancy in winter. All zoysias are slow-growing and require 1 to 3 years for development of a solid turf. A single edging-board will contain them. In warm summer areas, they are useful for shaded areas when the general lawn expanse is of hybrid Bermuda because they blend well with Bermuda in texture and color. Same general care. They are more durable when dormant than other warm-season grasses.
	MEYER	Blades broad at base, tapering to point at tips. Established turf looks much like top quality bluegrass lawn.	Improves with age. Underground root system. Drought and weed-resistant. Pest-free. Most wear-resistant. Easy to maintain. Soft to walk on in bare feet. Takes intense playground punishment. Spreads rapidly. Very winter hardy.	Coarser than those below. Winter color is brown vs. straw color for those below.	Goes off color early—greens up late in spring.	Seeds or stolons, plugs, solid.	Fair	Low, ½ inch.	
	Z. MATRELLA	Medium fine texture. Slick, slightly bristly, dense. Similar in appearance to bluegrass.	Easy to maintain. Wear-resistant. Holds color better than Meyer Zoysia.	Has some viable seed which does not always come true.	Turns straw color in winter, but not as scraggly looking when dormant as Bermuda. May hold fair color during mild winter.	"	Yes, in areas with warm summer nights.	"	
	EMERALD	Wiriest of zoysias. Denser than Meyer. Darker green. More prickly than any other zoysia.	Easy to maintain. Grows more slowly than Meyer. Good wear-resistance. Dense, wiry blades make cutting difficult.	Not as even-textured, tends to grow in whorls, but they can be eliminated with close mowing.	More frost-tolerant than other zoysias and Bermudas. Stays green in frost-free areas.	Sprigs, plugs, solid.	"	"	

Evaluation of subtropical grasses (continued)

	What does it look like?	What are its good points?	What are its bad points?	Winter color retention?	How to plant: Seeds, sprigs, or stolons?	Does it grow in shade?	Best with high or lower mowing?	Comments on the entire genus or class.
ST. AUGUSTINE GRASS								
ST. AUGUSTINE GRASS	Coarse. Very wide blades. Dark green.	Planted away from other grasses so you can't notice its comparative coarseness, it makes an attractive, rugged, serviceable lawn. Completely pest-free. Salt tolerant.	Coarse texture makes power mower a necessity. Creeps into flower beds, but is shallow rooted and therefore easier to get out. Produces very thick thatch.	Turns brown if it gets any frost. But its brown season is shorter than that of Bermudas.	Flats or plugs of sod, or stolons or sprigs.	Yes, if not too dense. Best shade grass for warm climates.	Cut at ½ to 1½ inches.	
BERMUDA GRASSES								
COMMON	The grayish green Bermuda grass with the bronzy seed spikes, that seemingly grows everywhere in Bermuda grass areas.	In Bermuda grass areas it volunteers and makes a comparatively pest-free and disease-free lawn if well tended. Can be overseeded with "winter grass."	Coarser than any of the hybrids listed below. More seed spikes. Inclined to grow lumpy.	Brown or straw-colored all winter (December through March in Los Angeles).	Hulled seeds or sprigs. (Unhulled seed may remain dormant for years.)	No	As low as you can set your mower (½ inch if possible).	This is the original garden lawn Bermuda. Prettier if fertilized regularly, but because of bad seeding habits and invasive growth, it is not a perfect lawn grass.
U-3	Finer textured than Common, coarser than most other hybrids. Seed spikes just as obvious as on Common.	Tough enough for athletic fields. Tends to build up instead of out. Result is less invasion but more thatch.	From seed, it is not always dependable — may revert to many different types. Less aggressive, so worn spots may fill back with Common Bermuda.	Browns off about same time as Common.	Stolons or sprigs only for true U-3.	"	"	
EVERGLADES #3 or ORMOND	Medium-textured and a bright, deep green. Soft feeling.	Rapid coverage from sprigs or plugs. Exceptionally nice color. Good for heavy play areas. Very vigorous recovery after mechanical damage.	Requires more frequent mowing than U-3, Sunturf, or Tifgreen. A preferred host of Bermuda mite.	One of the best for winter color retention. Does brown out for slight period.	Stolons or sprigs.	"	"	
TIFGREEN	Fine-textured, deep blue-green, dense.	Outstanding hybrid Bermuda for home lawns in general. Because blades grow out at soil level, can mow very close. Made to order for putting green. Less seed spikes. Sterile (no seeds).	May be a preferred host of some insect pests because of softness. Susceptible to smog damage.	Shorter dormant (brown) period than most hybrid Bermudas.	"	"	"	And these are the new hybrids—each considered an improvement on one count or another. All will crowd out Common Bermuda. Best adapted grasses for all areas of the Southwest. More difficult to overseed with "winter-grass." (bluegrass, red fescue, rye) than Common Bermuda. Winter green is assisted by fertilization in September and October and removal of thatch, which insulates the grass from the warm soil by September 1st.
T-35-A	Fine-textured, dense, light green, upright leaf growth.	Fast coverage.	Does not take traffic as well as other hybrids. Turf not as dense as other hybrid Bermudas. Grows too fast for home use.	Not as good as the three varieties directly above.	"	"	"	
TIFFINE	One of the finest textures. Yellow-green color.	Resists weeds well.	Produces masses of seed heads during most of summer—not generally recommended for California.	Poor	"	"	"	
SUNTURF	Along with Tifgreen, it is the finest textured lawn grass we've seen. It's almost like Irish moss in texture. Dark green.	Its fine texture and wear-resistance are its best points. Probably can take cold weather better than any other hybrid Bermuda. Sterile (no seeds).	A red pigment develops when cool temperatures arrive, giving lawn a reddish purple coat.	More evergreen than U-3 but does brown out for short period.	"	"	"	
TIFWAY	Prostrate growth, fine texture, stiff blades, dark green color.	Very dense, wear resistant. Excellent color. Sterile (no seeds).	Tends to grow in whorls. Slower than others to establish.	Good	"	"	"	

How to Install a Lawn

One thing all fine lawns have in common is an adequate soil for the roots to grow in. This is as true of a fine-looking Kentucky bluegrass lawn in Seattle or Boston as it is of a fine-looking hybrid Bermuda lawn in Santa Barbara or St. Petersburg.

Each of the pre-planting steps described here is generally recognized as being essential to building a lawn that will perform for many years to come. You can short-cut the installation procedure with abandon if you want a lawn of temporary nature, if the lawn you are building can be second or third-rate in quality, or if you live in an especially favored climate.

Making a good lawn the right way is not easy. But each step in the process leads to avoiding a familiar short-coming of bad, old lawns. For instance, careful grading makes good drainage so your lawn won't puddle and develop spots that are waterlogged and soft, or hard and dry. Incorporating organic matter and other soil amendments gives you a lawn that's easy to maintain. Blending topsoil with native soil to make a transitional layer between topsoil and native soil avoids trapping roots in a shallow topsoil basin in which they would be dependent on frequent feeding and very frequent watering.

The structure of your soil will affect the ease of installation and will influence your later habits in watering and feeding the lawn after it comes up. If your soil is dense and drains poorly, you can probably profit by mixing it thoroughly with 30 to 50 percent by volume of a porous soil amendment, as described on pages 17, 18.

ABOUT SCALPING OLD LAWNS

The photo on this page shows one way to remove a bad, old lawn in order to begin making a new one. Another method, to be used in communities where there are no power sod-cutters for rent, is to strip off the old sod with a flat-back spade. One way or the other, you should remove old sod before building a new lawn. Don't dig existing sod into soil. Clumps of buried sod make for poor rooting, erratic water penetration, and uneven settling (a bumpy surface).

POWER SOD CUTTER makes easy job of removing sod before making new lawn. Old sod should not be spaded under. Remove with a spade if you can't rent cutter

Some good reasons for removing an old lawn and starting over: the old lawn contains noxious weed grasses such as Bermuda grass (see page 56 for how to kill Bermuda thoroughly before you slice it off); it has humps or hollows; water penetration is poor; or you wish to install a complex sprinkling system requiring much digging.

ADD TOPSOIL ONLY IF YOU MUST RAISE THE GRADE

If your lawn area's surface is lower than you want it ("below grade" in landscape architects' parlance), and must be filled in, you will have to add introduced soil. This should be the only reason for adding topsoil. When you buy topsoil, you are pretty much at the mercy of the man who's selling it.

There are no specifications for topsoil. Two things you should look for: crumbly texture; lack of salinity (if it comes from an area where crop growth was good, you can assume that its salinity is adequately low). You can buy topsoil through your nurseryman, through landscape contractors, or soil dealers (listed in the classified telephone directory under the heading TOPSOIL).

Addition of topsoil can be rather tricky, especially if the new soil differs much from your native soil.

You won't run into much trouble if you add topsoil to an 8 to 12-inch depth. That much can hold grass roots fairly comfortably.

Trouble comes with a layer of introduced topsoil that is 4, 6, or 8 inches deep lying above a soil of a different texture. Water may back up at the plane where the old and new soils meet, and roots will not grow through to their best depth. To get around this, make a blend between the two layers. Add half the total amount of topsoil you are going to need, spade it into the native soil to make an even mix. Then add the rest of the topsoil to bring the level up to grade.

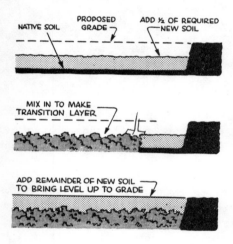

NATIVE SOIL — PROPOSED GRADE — ADD ½ OF REQUIRED NEW SOIL

MIX IN TO MAKE TRANSITION LAYER

ADD REMAINDER OF NEW SOIL TO BRING LEVEL UP TO GRADE

EXTREME ACID OR ALKALINE CONDITION

An extreme acid or alkaline condition in a soil will limit availability of some nutrients and thereby limit a lawn's performance in it.

Ordinarily, most gardeners are well aware of any extreme condition in their soil. Old-timers in the neighborhood can tell you what the typical soil in the area is like. Generally speaking, highly acid soils are found in high rainfall areas whereas alkaline problem soils are found in arid places.

If you want to find out exactly where your soil measures in the acid-alkaline scale, you can test it with a soil-testing kit, or send a soil sample to a testing laboratory for analysis. Dig up trowel-size samples from the top 6 inches of soil from widely scattered spots throughout the lawn area. Mix the samples together thoroughly with the trowel (keep your hands out of the soil sample as much as possible), let it dry in the air, and place about a pint of the mixed soil in a light, sturdy mailing container, such as a coffee can. Label it and attach to the shipping carton a first-class letter containing details. Where to send it? Look in your telephone book or ask your County Agent for the name of a nearby laboratory that will test soil. In some states, County Agricultural Agents themselves will test soil for residents of their counties.

To correct an undesirable condition:

1. If your soil is acid enough to limit growth (pH below 5.5), neutralize it by applying lime (ground dolomite limestone is best form; don't use hydrated lime) at the rate of 50 to 75 pounds per 1,000 square feet per application. The lime decreases soil acidity by direct chemical action. Apply on dry soil with a spreader. Prevent chemical from contacting roots of acid-loving shrubs.

2. If you have alkaline soil, you can use one of several products to reduce the alkalinity and at the same time improve soil structure. Actually, you should strive to lower pH only if it is above 8.3 or 8.4. Gypsum is the most widely used for this purpose. In areas where water companies soften the water supply, gypsum is the best way to prevent a "tight" soil. It has the advantage of practically limitless safe application. Spread as much as you wish on top of the soil (the usual recommendation is "like a light snow") and spade it in. About 35 to 50 pounds per 1,000 square feet will usually suffice.

MIX NUTRIENTS INTO ROOTING AREA

The three plant food elements most needed by a lawn (or any other garden plants) are nitrogen, phosphorus, and potash. These elements and the need for them are fully discussed in the lawn fertilizing chapter on pages 60 to 64.

As you will see in the fertilizing chapter, a lawn will need applications of fertilizer containing nitrogen continually. You cannot possibly apply enough nitrogen fertilizer to last the lawn's lifetime when you prepare the rooting area. But, you can supply enough at that time to sustain the young grass right after it germinates. In the section that follows, about mixing organic soil amendments into the soil, several provisions are given for supplying nitrogen. If you choose not to follow any of these suggestions, you can broadcast or spread any fertilizer containing nitrogen over the completed seedbed when you sow the seed. Follow directions on the fertilizer package label.

In contrast to the nitrogen that will be needed continually, your only chance to supply phosphate fertilizer to the subsurface rooting area is at the time you cultivate the soil. Before you cultivate, evenly spread 40 pounds of single superphosphate per 1,000 square feet. The subsequent cultivating will mix it thoroughly throughout the rooting area.

Here are some other plant food elements to add *before cultivating* under certain circumstances:

In some parts of the country that get considerable rainfall, such as western Oregon and Washington, added potash is often needed in the rooting area for good turf growth. It's seldom needed in arid climates. Ask your County Agricultural Agent or other local expert about the need for potash if you are in doubt. Where it is needed, apply evenly to the surface and mix thoroughly into the rooting area 10 pounds of muriate of potash to each 1,000 square feet.

When large quantities of sawdust are added to soils (see next section), use an iron-supplying material (iron sulfate or iron chelate) to avoid iron chlorosis symptoms. Iron sulfate is most used, but keep it off concrete; if wet, it red-stains permanently. Use 5 to 10 pounds of it per 1,000 square feet in pre-planting, or 5 pounds over the same area on existing lawns. Follow label directions for chelates.

APPLY NUTRIENTS that are to be tilled into the soil. Weigh amounts to be mixed into each 1,000 square feet and scatter them evenly over measured areas

THREE-INCH LAYER of sawdust spread on surface before being cultivated into top 6 inches of soil will make recommended 33 percent by volume of sawdust

IMPROVE SOIL AERATION WITH QUANTITIES OF ORGANIC SOIL AMENDMENT

From California comes a new lawn-making technique that has proved to be most satisfactory for building a lawn bed. With this method, you make a lawn that will take water easily (no runoff), and hold it so that watering intervals can be lengthened considerably during the long dry season.

The basic innovation is the addition to the native soil of 30 to 50 percent by volume of porous soil amendment to supply air spaces in the soil and improve water penetration. Even if you start with a poor soil, results indicate that this method is much better and no more expensive than the procedure of hauling in topsoil.

Any material that in itself is a good plant-growing medium, when water and plant food are added, can be considered a good soil amendment for the new kind of lawn described here.

On basis of cost, availability, and measured success, the best choice for this purpose is sawdust (any kind that decomposes slowly, is uniform in texture, and not toxic) or ground bark. By shopping at dealers that offer these materials in bulk, you can often buy what you need quite reasonably.

If you use raw sawdust or ground bark, you must mix nitrogen fertilizer with it because the soil organisms that work to decompose wood products require nitrogen as fuel. Otherwise, until the sawdust breaks down, your soil bed would be nitrogen deficient.

> For each 1,000 square feet of sawdust or ground bark, laid 3 inches deep, mix in 55 pounds of ammonium sulfate or 35 pounds of ammonium nitrate.

As another choice, look for nitrogen-treated sawdust

CULTIVATE sawdust (or similar material) thoroughly into the soil. It requires many trips back and forth with the tiller to blend a homogenous mixture

ROLL one direction with a heavy roller, then roll crosswise. This picture shows the first rolling, when the tilled mixture of sawdust and soil is still soft

or ground bark. These products require no extra nitrogen.

There's a third choice, and it's a two-birds-with-one-stone scheme. Use calcium cyanamid. Apply 25 pounds of it per 1,000 square feet before spreading and blending in the soil amendment, and follow with subsequent steps described on page 19. This chemical is a nitrogen compound that cooks weed seeds to death, then dissipates. Enough nitrogen remains first to feed the soil organisms that work on the sawdust or ground bark and then to feed the young grass you've planted. The calcium cyanamid treatment calls for an extra 30 days (less in hot weather) of daily sprinkling before you sow your grass seed.

Three inches of the soil amendment mixed with the top 6 inches of soil makes a 33 percent mix.

The soil amendment must be mixed uniformly and completely with the soil. Use a big, powerful rotary tiller and make many repeated passes at all sections, tilling and blending until you have created a homogeneous mixture.

MAKING THE LAWN BED SMOOTH

A lawn bed should be as smooth and flat as possible. However, it should have a slight pitch, even in flatland gardens. Figure on a fall of 6 to 12 inches in 100 feet so that water can run off once the root area has reached its saturation point. Only about one lawn in fifty requires drain tile to take off the excess.

For most suburban homeowners, such talk is academic because the elevations of surrounding paving dictate the lawn grade and pitch it to an adequate slope.

If you blend in the 30 to 50 percent by volume of porous soil amendment, as outlined on page 17, you may find the mixture piled too high around the edges when you begin to level. If so, do this: spade off excess around

THIS DEVICE does a fine job of reducing the high spots and filling in the low spots on both the push and pull strokes. Use it between and after rollings

the edges, and throw it to the center, level and roll, do it again if necessary. Ultimately this will form a slight center crown.

In the rare instances where driveways and existing paving do not dictate the lawn's grade and pitch, you should establish a high side and a low side by means of level line or other device; mark these points on stakes.

One way or the other, your aim will be to drag the cultivated soil until it is flat, free of clods, and conforming to grade or desired pitch. You can make a good drag for first leveling by overlapping a series of planks so that the drag rides on the down-facing exposed edges, as illustrated.

The drag will cut off the high spots and fill in the low spots. A "window frame" drag (four timbers in a square frame with a weight on top of it) will, when pulled horizontally along loose soil, pick up a high spot and deposit it in a low. You can put on a finished smooth surface with a straight-edge of 1-by-6 lumber about 4 feet across, mounted as the top of a T on a 2-by-2 handle about 8 or 10 feet long.

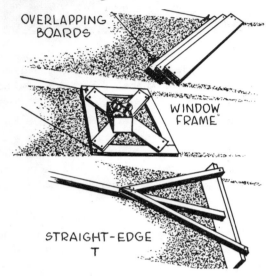

OVERLAPPING BOARDS

WINDOW FRAME

STRAIGHT-EDGE T

A rectangle of flexible steel matting, 3 feet by 5 feet, makes a wonderful smoothing and leveling device.

To firm the seedbed, go over the smoothed surface in two directions with a full roller. The heavy rolling process may develop some low spots. If it does, fill them in with another raking or dragging, and roll again.

FOLLOW-UP STEPS IF YOU USE CALCIUM CYANAMID

As the second phase of the calcium cyanamid treatment (one of the means of supplying nitrogen for the sawdust or other woody material suggested on page 17): spread 35 pounds of calcium cyanamid per 1,000 square feet evenly over the finished surface. Determine the proper fertilizer spreader setting by spreading the material on a large sheet of paper, weighing the amount caught, and matching the weight against the area of paper covered.

After spreading, rake in two directions to blend the material with the surface 1/4 to 1/2 inch. Most of the weed seeds upon which the calcium cyanamid should act are those that end up in the top 1/2 inch.

If trees or deep rooted (old, big) shrubs grow in the lawn area, there's no danger in using this product. Along the side, do not treat areas in which shallow roots of nearby shrubs may grow.

Soak the treated area after raking and keep the soil moist (sprinkle daily) for 30 days. Water makes the chemical act on weed seeds, then lose its potency so grass seed can grow. In warm weather the chemical dissipates in less time. You can test to see if the calcium cyanamid has safely dissipated by sowing radish seed on the soil. They germinate in just a few days. If they begin to form leaves, the soil is safe for grass seed.

SEEDING A PREPARED LAWN BED

We speak here of how best to sow seed of the cool-season or hardy grasses on ground prepared as suggested on the previous pages. Although lawn seed may be sown in almost any month in warmer parts of the country and from spring through fall in the cooler regions, fall and spring are accepted as the best times.

Fall sowing is preferred by most experienced lawn installers because the lower temperatures reduce danger of heat injury (most grasses prefer to grow at temperatures between 50° and 70°). Fall seeding should be done early enough to allow 6 weeks of growth before heavy frosts come and the soil gets cold. Grass sown too late in fall may not germinate at all; or an early heavy rain might wash out the seedbed.

Grass sown in spring will get the benefit of months of heat, which if combined with ample water, will make for luxuriant growth. Main weakness of spring planting is the travail of bringing a new lawn through the heat of summer and through the season of most active weed growth.

Broadcast the seed on the prepared lawn bed while the air is quiet.

Here is a way to get the seed on uniformly: divide the amount of seed necessary for your area (per label direction on seed packages) into four equal portions, so you can make four approaches over the seedbed. Divide the seedbed in half by running a string down the middle. Broadcast one quarter portion down each half, spreading

SOW SEED with a mechanical spreader of some sort. Hand seeding is often uneven. Here the seed is being deposited reasonably even with a fertilizer spreader

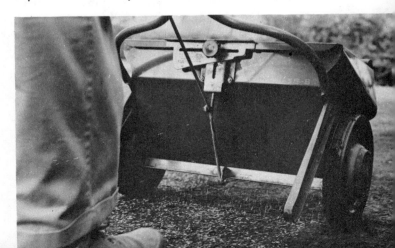

RAKE and cross-rake the newly-sown seed to bond it with the soil. You don't have to press down hard — just lightly scratch or brush the seeded surface

SEED MULCH is necessary (where hot, dry weather can be expected) to help keep seed and young seedlings continually moist. Dampened peat moss used here

it evenly and uniformly within each marked area. Then run string across the middle of the lawn in the opposite direction and scatter the remaining two quarter portions on these two halves.

You can broadcast the seed uniformly with a mechanical seeder.

After the seed is broadcast, rake it in lightly to insure a thorough contact of seed with seedbed soil. Very lightly brush up the seeded surface with a wire rake— use light circular motions, straight motions, or whatever appears to disperse the seed most evenly for you. If you come across concentrated patches of seeds, in spite of your care, swirl them out lightly into the surrounding area to make an even coverage. At this stage, your heels may make an undesirable impression in the seedbed— try doing the cross-raking and mulching in flat-soled shoes, tennis shoes, or barefooted.

If you can expect hot, dry weather or drying winds in the 30 days after sowing, it's a good idea to apply a thin, moisture-holding mulch over the seed. After seeding and cross-raking, put on a 1/8 to 3/16-inch layer of peat moss or screened sawdust that has been aged at least a year. Scatter the mulch on as evenly as possible. Don't toss it upward so that it falls in piles.

Many people find peat moss troublesome because of its reluctance to take up water. Most reliable method—

and also the most tedious—is to pre-soak the peat before applying it. Break off chunks into a wheelbarrow and pulverize them; then slowly add water and knead it into the peat until it is thoroughly saturated. A non-ionic wetting agent added to the water will speed the pre-soaking.

Whatever the covering, roll it smooth with a light roller (empty) after you have applied it. If a peat moss covering is lumpy, chop up the lumps with the backside of a wire rake before rolling.

For initial watering, you will need adequate hose to get all the way around your lawn without dragging across it, and a hand sprinkler that throws out a thorough but gentle spray. You will also need up to half an hour a day for 20 to 30 days for watering. When days are warm and windy you may have to water 2 or 3 times a a day to keep the surface continually wet. Keep the top dark with moisture until all the grasses are up. This may take up to three weeks if your seed mix includes slow-germinating varieties. Don't use a set sprinkler on a lawn seedbed. If you have a well-designed underground system, you can use it to bring the grass up, but cease and sprinkle by hand or use a plastic hose sprinkler if the underground system causes washouts.

If seed and mulch happen to wash off onto an adjoining paved area, don't attempt to blast them back into

WATERING will become familiar chore. If any portion of the bed is allowed to dry out on top, the germinating seeds or young seedlings in that spot will die

WALK ON PLANK to pull emerging weeds after a week or two. Get them while they are small. Or wait 6 to 8 weeks and use a broad leafed weed killer

place with the spray — you may wash out more seeds along the side of the seedbed.

After the first week, the little seedlings will have gained enough stature to take a bending. It is possible, and often advisable at that time, to pull the weeds that come up with the seeds. Lay a plank out across the seedbed and walk along it to pull the weeds.

Where labor is being paid, weeding is often skipped. Instead, a broad-leafed weed killer (see page 50) is applied to the lawn after the second or third mowing. These weed killers can kill young grasses; be sure to observe label precautions.

Mow the lawn for the first time when the grass is about two inches high. One sensible recommendation says mow when the grass blades get tall enough to take on a noticeable curvature. Bent grasses that are to be cut at 1 inch high should never be allowed to grow much higher than 1 inch. It is important that the mower be sharp at all times. Dull blades can just mangle and pull up lightly anchored seedlings by the roots.

SEEDING ON A SLOPE

Lawns can be planted successfully on ground that slopes up to 15 per cent. If the slope is steeper, a ground cover or a system of terraces would be more satisfactory.

Prepare the seedbed as described in the steps for planting a lawn on flat ground, with the following special care: When you rake the seedbed, rake across the slope. When you roll the seedbed, roll it up and down. Burlap or a specially manufactured anti-erosion net spread over a newly seeded slope will keep moisture in the ground and prevent seed from washing away. If the burlap is of a tight weave, remove it as soon as the grass begins to come up. Anti-erosion net or loose-weave burlap can be left in place to rot. You can use your sprinkler system if you cover the slope with burlap and cut holes for the sprinkler heads. Otherwise, you should water the seedbed by hand, standing at the bottom of the slope if possible, and water from the bottom to the top. Don't use sprinklers for at least two weeks, and then run them slowly to avoid puddling and washouts.

If erosion is likely to be a problem, you should install a drain scupper across the top of the slope to carry water off to one side.

Sodding with desired permanent grasses is a good solution where an immediate erosion hazard exists.

SODDING A PREPARED LAWN BED

In the midwest and east, lawn grass has been sold in sod sections for as long as anyone can remember. Home-owners buy some sod from a farmer, who cuts it and rolls it up from his all-year-green pasture. Some dealers there offer sod of certain kinds of lawn grasses.

On the West Coast, until quite recently, sodding was looked upon as another practice exclusive to the east. In recent years, sodding has come to that part of the west. Turf farms there are growing selected kinds of turf plants (dichondra and grasses) in fields that are maintained as king-sized lawns the year around — fertilized, watered, mowed, sprayed. This grass is sold to home-owners from beautifully maintained, selected-variety lawns.

Wherever you live, this is the planting method: Prepare soil as outlined on pages 15 to 19. But, instead of working toward a finished soil grade at the level of surrounding paving, the soil surface should be settled ¾-inch below grade.

Some lawn contractors say you get a much better take-off if you spread a layer of complete fertilizer (label-prescribed amount for new lawns) on the soil and lay the sod directly on it.

Unroll the sod on the prepared soil. Lay the strips parallel with the strip ends staggered as in the brick-layers' running bond pattern. Press each successively laid strip snugly up against the one next to it.

After the sod strips are all laid in this fashion, roll the sod with a roller half full of water to smooth out rough spots and bond the sod with the soil.

Now all you have to do is water a little more carefully than usual for a few days. Aside from that, it is as if the lawn has been yours, maintained with great care, for years. In just a few hours, you get a mature lawn.

You avoid the tedious sprinkling two or three times a day that is necessary when you sow, sprig, or plug a new lawn. There is no early weeding because there is no bare soil for weeds to germinate and grow in.

Many home gardeners will get a better lawn in the long run from good, weed-free sod, professionally installed, than from seed, sprigs, or plugs, simply because the turf farmers produce a denser and healthier lawn than does a home gardener who might be indifferent, inept, or inexperienced.

Growers charge a high price for sodded lawn. For comparative jobs (same sites and same type lawns) the price is about 10 cents per square foot more than for sowing, plugging, or sprigging a lawn. But for the extra 10 cents (an extra $100 in the case of a 1,000 square foot lawn) you get the advantages mentioned above.

MAKE FURROWS for planting stolons about 2 inches wide, 3 inches deep, and 10 inches apart. Or, space the furrows closer together to get a faster coverage

PRESS SOIL back firmly over the roots and other white parts of the stolons. Make surface smooth again. Soak the furrow. Here, the back part is planted

SPRIGGING AND BROADCASTING STOLONS ON A PREPARED LAWN BED

This consists of tearing apart clumps of the grass stems to get pieces an inch or two long, each carrying a few tufts of leaves. In some cases, the stems are torn apart from nursery flats or from growing grass in nursery areas. As another method, you buy plastic bags of sprigs that were dug, cleaned, separated, and sent from the growers by air freight in the 24 hours or so before planting.

The time to plant sprigs or stolons of Bermuda and other subtropical grasses is late spring or summer.

First, pre-soak the prepared planting bed so it will be damp when you plant the stolons or sprigs. When it is dry enough to work without sticking, make a series of parallel trenches 3 inches deep, and 10 inches apart.

Plant individual stolons vertically in trenches and press the soil together by putting pressure beside the trench. Water the sprigged area soon after planting, and keep it moist continually until the sprigs have rooted and begun to grow.

Although lawn establishment by sprigs is fast, an easier way is to broadcast the stolons. This is not new,

but it is coming into use more for Bermudas, zoysias, and bent grasses. After the lawn bed surface is prepared, scatter pieces of stems (stolons) by hand over the entire area. Approximately 3 to 5 bushels should cover 1,000 square feet.

Roll the entire planting with a half-filled lawn roller to firm the stolons against the soil surface.

After broadcasting and rolling, cover the stem pieces with some material that will hold moisture well during the rooting. This might be a half-inch of screened, weed-free topsoil, peat moss, sawdust, or ground bark. The latter two materials should be thoroughly pre-soaked, as they are very difficult to wet through when applied dry. Roll again after applying the layer of cover material, to insure that it is in firm contact with the stolons.

Water immediately after the second rolling. Thereafter, water the mulched surface frequently (maybe several times a day in warm weather) so that it will not dry out at any time. Of all ways to start Bermuda, this one calls for most painstaking maintenance after planting.

PLUGGING A PREPARED LAWN BED

Cut and lift plugs of the new grass from flats with a special plugging tool ($1\frac{1}{2}$ inches in diameter and 3 inches long). Then plant the plugs in small holes made in the prepared lawn area with the same plugging tool. As an extra, put a teaspoon of complete fertilizer in each hole before planting. It will make the grass grow faster. Plugs are usually spaced 12 to 15 inches apart.

Growth from plugs may be fast, but somewhat slower than with sprigging. Plugging is most frequently used for planting hybrid Bermuda and dichondra (more plugging instructions are given in the dichondra chapter, page 78).

PLACE STOLONS or runners against the back of the trench so that the green grass blades will be above grade level and all of the white parts will be below

Efficient Lawn Watering

Whenever you see a lawn that is green and lush every day through the summer months, you'll find a gardener with an efficient watering system. The system may be built on personal observation, or it may have been figured out scientifically and mathematically. It may call for watering every other day, or once in 10 days. Regardless of what the schedule is and how it was arrived at, it will be based on many things—rate of water penetration, water capacity of the soil, depth of topsoil, depth of grass roots, rate of water loss by evaporation and transpiration, appearance of grass. Let's take a look at each factor.

WATER PENETRATION

If you have sandy soil, you can pour on the water and it will disappear immediately. With many heavy clay soils, water penetrates so slowly that the average sprinkler will put water on faster than the soil will take it. Long before the soil is satisfied, you'll have small lakes or run-off into driveways, flower beds, or street.

SOIL CAPACITY

Each soil type has its own water holding capacity. The larger the soil particles, the less will be its water holding capacity.

Here's the capacity of 100 square feet of soil, 1 foot deep:

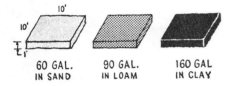

60 GAL. IN SAND   90 GAL. IN LOAM   160 GAL IN CLAY

Obviously the lighter soil must be watered more frequently than the heavy soil in order to keep moisture in it. If plants in each area were extracting 60 gallons a week, you would have to water sand once a week, loam every 10½ days, clay every 2½ weeks.

ROOT DEPTHS

Most people think that grass roots grow about 3 to 6 inches down into the soil. When you cut into a lawn with a spade, thickness of the turf seems to be the root depth. Actually, when you spade out a section of turf, you break off the long hair-like roots that may grow down far below the obvious surface roots.

In good deep soil, grass roots will go down to from 24 to 30 inches, depending upon the type of grass, its age (surprisingly, a lawn's root system goes deepest during the first year or two), and how the soil is watered.

SAND 120 GAL.   LOAM 180 GAL.   CLAY 320 GAL.

In deep soil, therefore, you are working with this possibility: A root-filled block of soil 10 feet by 10 feet on the surface and 2 feet or more deep acts as a water reservoir of 120 to 320 gallons, depending upon the soil type.

BUT SOIL IS NOT ALWAYS DEEP

All the figures on root depths and water holding capacity mean nothing if the topsoil is underlaid with a layer of soil that is impervious to water. For example, some soil profiles look like this:

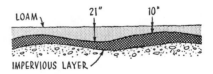

LOAM   21"   10"   IMPERVIOUS LAYER

In situations of that kind where there are areas of both shallow and deep topsoil, you might as well set your water schedule to the shallow depth.

In many situations soil changes abruptly from one type of soil to another as you follow it down through the top 2 feet. A 12-inch sandy loam may be underlaid with clay. While this clay would take water if it were on the surface, water from the topsoil and roots in the topsoil may enter the clay layer only with difficulty. The same is true of clay over sand or any other abrupt change in profile—that is why it's so important to make the transition layer when you bring in topsoil (page 16).

RATE OF WATER LOSS

Water is lost from the soil by evaporation and transpiration. Transpiration (loss of water through plant surfaces) accounts for the major portion and increases with temperature, sunlight, and air movement. If a tree's roots grow in your lawn, remember that they also take water from the same soil. Three factors cause lawns to go partially bald under trees: shade; competition for nutrients; competition for water. Under trees you should feed the lawn twice as much (for the tree and the lawn) and water it considerably more than in open areas out from under trees.

A good stand of grass insulates the soil and reduces evaporation by sun or wind to the minimum.

The average water loss in mild-summer areas is about 1 inch of water each week. In the hot localities, especially when a dry wind is blowing, the weekly loss increases to 2 inches and more a week.

The observant gardener aims to replace the water loss. As rate of loss increases, he will either water more frequently or in a greater amount.

HOW DEEP DOES THE WATER GO?

In dry soil 1 inch of water will penetrate as follows:

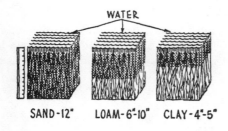

WATER

SAND-12"   LOAM-6"-10"   CLAY-4"-5"

Water does not move down through soil until each soil particle has its film of water. After each particle has its quota, the additional water is free to move on to the next particle.

How deep 1 inch of water will penetrate depends on the moisture in the soil when you apply the water.

For example, if you had an open field with a clay soil that was completely dried out by the time of a rain, it would have to receive 10 inches of rain before it became wet to a depth of 3 feet.

But an added inch of water would penetrate 3 feet and more if the first 3 feet were saturated.

In a lawn the grass root tips take from the film of water around the soil particles wherever there are roots.

APPEARANCE OF GRASS

Grass shows its need of water first by loss of resilience. When you walk across it, there is no springback; you can see your footprints in the grass.

Next, the color changes from fresh green and takes on an overcast of dull, gray-green smokiness, almost blue.

The grass tops begin to turn brown and die. Storage of some water in the roots keeps the crowns of the grass plants alive long after the tops die.

Ideally, you should water before even the no-springback sign comes along. After you live with a lawn for a while, you can sense such timing. But, there is no great danger if you water heavily right at the no-springback stage or even when grass has taken on the smoky color. Grass that has begun to turn brown from lack of water will take considerable time to come back.

WHY WEEKLY INSTEAD OF DAILY
OR EVERY OTHER DAY?

Stretching the interval between waterings to as many days as your lawn can take it has much in its favor.

Many gardeners, even in hot-summer areas, claim that alternate wetting and partial drying out of soil, encourage healthier plant growth and deeper rooting. As water is drawn from the soil by grass roots, more air enters and a better environment for growth is created.

Opponents of this argument contend that partial drying out makes the grass suffer during hot weather. They give their lawns a light sprinkling every afternoon or evening. This cools the garden and the people in it as much as it cools the grass, but this technique should never be looked upon as watering. It usually doesn't supply enough water to meet the grass plants' needs.

Deep watering once a week is safer than frequent watering from the angle of over-watering, too.

Weekly watering makes sense if the lawn is played on daily. Not only will there be fewer mud stains on clothing, but the surface of the soil will not be subject to compaction every day or so.

Weekly watering, when taken on as a 2 to 3-hour job, can take care of the unevenness of water application that is so hard to avoid with sprinklers. While you're weeding, pruning, or just puttering around the garden, you can run water slowly onto the hard spots and places that regular sprinklers do not reach. The slow soaking will make water penetrate as deep in those spots as it does elsewhere.

The deep watering at weekly intervals will help in situations where there are both tree and grass roots in the lawn area. By taking the time to soak the tree root area, you can do a lot to prevent the extension of tree roots into a wider and wider area of the lawn's surface.

In the arid West, where no rainfall comes for 6 to 9 months, the time to change from frequent-and-shallow watering to infrequent-and-deep is at the end of the rainy season. If you are already into the dry season, continue the practice until the next rainy season, since shallow rooting has already been established.

HOW THE FREQUENT SCHEDULE GETS YOU INTO TROUBLE

The University of California can be looked upon as a knowing spokesman on the subject of irrigation in arid (dry summer) climates. The University's watering recommendation for home lawns, in synopsis, goes like this: Water deeply with at least one-half to one inch at each irrigation, applied at intervals of once or at most twice a week, depending on soil, temperature, and kind of grass or ground cover.

Research by the University has shown that light watering every day or every other day has several disadvantages:
- Greater total water use.
- Shallow rooting.
- Severe drying of root system from a few days' neglect.
- Rapid build-up of salinity due to lack of leaching.
- Encouragement of shallow-rooted weeds, particularly crabgrass.
- Production of an environment favorable to disease.
- Compaction.
- Greater total water loss due to evaporation—expensive under some water rates.

HOW MUCH WATER DO YOU APPLY PER MINUTE OR PER HOUR?

One inch of water applied to 100 square feet of lawn is equal to 60 gallons. The average sprinkler with the average water pressure will deliver 5 gallons a minute. So if you use 1 sprinkler to cover a lawn area of 1,000 square feet, the sprinkler would have to run 2 hours to add an inch of water to the lawn.

In most localities 5 gallons a minute is about the average volume. You can figure your delivery rate from a hose by measuring the gallons per minute in a bucket.

Measure the amount of water delivered by a sprinkling system by placing containers around the lawn. This will also give you a clear picture of how equally your sprinkler distributes the water you send through it. You can find how long to run your sprinklers and what positions will wet your lawn most evenly.

You can put on more water in less time by increasing the size of hose you use. Just as the inside diameter of a water pipe determines the volume of water delivered (see sprinkler systems chapter), so does the inside diameter of a hose determine the amount of water that will go through it in any interval of time. At the bottom of pages 26 and 27 you will see an interesting demonstration of the volume of water delivered by the different size hoses, and how much they weigh when full of water (a meaningful consideration if you are going to pull the hoses around much).

HOW TO TEST THE DELIVERY OF PORTABLE SPRINKLERS

In preceding pages, you have read that a typical lawn needs 1 surface inch of water a week in cool, high humidity sections, and 2 inches in the hot, dry sections—and that this need continues all through the dry season.

Here is an easy way to figure how many minutes you must run your sprinkler to put 1 or 2 inches of water on your lawn. Place 4 or 5 coffee cans along a line running out from your sprinkler. Put the farthest can 15 to 20 feet out—that's about the limit of most portable sprinklers at usual domestic daytime water pressures. Turn on the water and note the time it takes to fill most of the test cans 1 inch or 2 inches—whichever your lawn demands.

Of course, the timing will be valid only at approximately the same time of day as you tested your sprinkler. In many cases pressure rises and falls during the day according to total neighborhood use of the water.

In addition to learning your sprinkler's rate of delivery, you will also see exactly what kind of water-spreading job your sprinkler does. You may be surprised at the unevenness of sprinkler delivery as compared to rain. (Sprinkler performance, in terms of wetting patterns, does not change much as pressure rises and falls.)

Perhaps your sprinkler soaks the inside of its circle or square and leaves the outside almost dry. It may put most of the water about 3 or 4 feet out from the sprinkler head. Or you may find that it makes a fairly even pattern over its entire diameter. If a wind is blowing and your sprinkler is the kind that makes some mist, you may find that as much as half the delivered water drifts off to one side, making a very lopsided pattern.

However, the sprinkler is certainly here to stay. Short

of rain, nothing does as good a job for the home garden. An engineered, permanent, underground system (see page 32) licks most of the portable sprinkler's shortcomings. But even with a portable sprinkler, you can do a much better job once you know how your particular sprinkler type spreads the water.

HOW SIGNIFICANT IS THE WETTING PATTERN?

For one thing, when you know the wetting pattern that your sprinkling system makes, you can figure out the best possible spots on your lawn to run the sprinkler in order to get even water penetration. An even dispersal of water will make for consistent root depth, and that helps keep grass uniform in appearance.

We know of lawns, watered with a portable sprinkler in the same spots each watering day, that show faded and sparse grass along the edges. The sprinkler drops very little water at the outside edge, so the roots there are shallow. The small amount of water doesn't penetrate very deep. The weak grass that manages to grow along the lawn's edges allows formation of all sorts of ugly weeds, such as dandelion, sorrel, and plantain, that can take less water than the typical lawn grass.

In spots that repeatedly get too much sprinkler water, you find such invaders as sedge (a thick-bladed, grassy-

---

A DEMONSTRATION OF THE VOLUMES DELIVERED AND THE WEIGHTS OF THE THREE HOSE SIZES

Garden hoses, as you can see by these photographs, come in different sizes—and in this instance, we mean *diameter,* an important consideration that many gardeners fail to comprehend until after they've made their purchase. The smallest diameter commonly sold—7/16 inch—is too small to be recommended for general gardening use, so we don't consider it here. Standard sizes are ½, ⅝, and ¾-inch diameter. A hose of 1-inch diameter is manufactured but it's seldom sold to home gardeners.

Regardless of what your water pressure happens to be, the output through a hose is in direct ratio to the hose's inside diameter. With water pressure of 50 pounds per square inch, a 50-foot length of ¾-inch hose would put an inch of water on a 1,500 square foot lawn in 39 minutes; the ⅝-inch size in 1 hour; the ½-inch size in 2 hours.

But a hose's weight is a factor to consider, too. The lower row of pictures shows the weight of the three hose sizes, empty and full. As you see there, for the fast delivery supplied by the biggest size, you must work harder to move it around and you have to give it more storage room, too, because a 50-foot length of the big size in a coil takes up about twice as much space as 50 feet of the small size in a coil.

When you buy a hose, avoid the super-bargains—they seldom last very long, and can cause you much trouble and lost time. The best indication of a good hose is a guarantee. Don't buy one that isn't guaranteed or warranteed. It's that simple.

In 15 seconds a ½-inch hose delivers this much . . .

In 15 seconds, a 50-foot length of ½-inch hose filled this 5-gallon jar approximately ⅓ full. Compare this delivery to that of the larger sizes, at right.

½-INCH: 6 pounds empty . . . and 9 pounds full

looking weed that thrives on swampy conditions), crab-grass, chickweed, annual bluegrass (a weedy grass), and possibly some summer fungus troubles caused by excess water. If bent grass is in a mixture, it can become a weed in heavily watered spots. In shady places or where light intensities are low, moss can form in overly wet areas.

The best answer to unequal water distribution is to relocate sprinkler positions so that wetting patterns overlap to make an equal coverage—if that's possible. In other instances, your best bet might be to supplement one sprinkler type with another that makes a compatible pattern. You will want to figure ways to minimize wetting of sidewalks, driveways, and house when you water the lawn.

On the following pages we show you 5 basic wetting patterns, which were made by 10 different sprinkler types which we tested on *Sunset's* level lawn.

Our 10 readings by no means represent an exhaustive test of sprinkler performance, since there are scores of different kinds of sprinklers (dozens of new ones come on the market each year). We picked 10 popular units, however, which do represent most of the basic types of sprinkler manufactured and used today.

. . . a ⅝-inch hose almost twice as much

Now we move to the next larger size. A 50-foot length of ⅝-inch hose, in the same brief period of time, filled the 5-gallon jar about ⅔ full.

. . . a ¾-inch hose fills the 5-gallon jar

Here, a 50-foot length of ¾-inch hose fills the 5-gallon jar in 15 seconds. This is the biggest size hose commonly sold.

⅝-INCH: 7½ pounds empty . . . and 13 pounds full

¾-INCH: 11 pounds empty . . . and 19½ pounds full

FIVE BASIC WETTING PATTERNS

The five wetting patterns described on these pages pretty well represent the performance of portable sprinklers in general. The pattern your sprinkler makes will probably jibe with one of those we picture here. A study of the pattern should help you decide how to make the most efficient use of your sprinkler. Don't count on lateral water movement to correct poor sprinkler coverage. If you've ever irrigated vegetables in a furrow, you know that water seldom moves sidewise very far underground. A soaker or a plastic sprinkler tube at low pressure can soak a lawn edge if the sprinkler doesn't do it adequately.

Wetting Pattern A:
An Even Spread if You Overlap

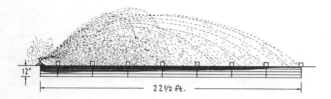

12"

22½ ft.

CROSS SECTION shows how pattern penetrates in loam. Penetration is deeper in sand, shallower in clay

Pattern A—Much water drops on the inside, and the amount diminishes slowly and evenly to the outside of the wetted area. A dispersal like this can make one of the most useful wetting patterns.

The 2 of our 10 sprinklers that made this wetting pattern were:

(1) The "impulse" or "machine gun" type, in which rapid-fire jets of water move around a circle and swing back again. Large models are used to irrigate crops.

(2) The slowly oscillating type with a horizontal bow arm that moves from side to side to deliver water over a rectangular or square area.

The reason this pattern is so valuable is obvious when you match up two such patterns, side by side. One can overlap the other exactly halfway to make one consistent soaking level—just as a couple of 30°-60° draftsman's triangles fitted together will make a rectangle.

Both of the sprinklers that made this pattern for us can be adjusted to take advantage of the overlap idea without wetting the sidewalk, driveway, or house. You can set the machine gun type from the 4 corners of a square or rectangle and adjust it each time to fit within the boundaries and do a good job of spreading water evenly (adjustments are explained below). The oscillating bow arm sprinkler is adjustable to make any size rectangle. You can even fix it so that it sprays only to one side. Accordingly, you could set one of these up with the one-sided adjustment in operation at each side of a rectangular lawn and the inward-directed spray patterns should overlap neatly.

Almost everything is adjustable on the machine gun type sprinkler head. You adjust two little sets of stops to make the arc cover any portion of a circle. Or you can line the stops up and let the sprinkler cover a full circle. On some models, you adjust a little jet-breaker pin or other deflector device to make long, thin streams or squashed-out sprays. We found on our model that adjusting the jet-breaker to make a straight stream made the sprinkler dump most of its water at the outside per-

PATTERN A. The "impulse" type of oscillating sprinkler, which is shown here in action, was one of two sprinklers tested that made a wetting pattern like this. Water diminishes evenly to outside of the wetted area

imeter, and that's seldom a useful pattern. But, deflector adjusted to break up the jet, it made a very even pattern, gradually diminishing to the outside.

One warning about the swinging bow arm sprinkler:

On the one we used, the high-trajectory jets were subject to drift in wind. You will get the most even distribution if you run such a sprinkler in the early morning or at other times when the air is still.

Wetting Pattern B:
You Make Successive Overlaps

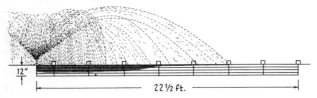

12"   22½ Ft.

WATER DISTRIBUTED this way causes mired spot in center, dry area at perimeter. Patterns must overlap

Pattern B—Much water drops on the inside, but it decreases fast in distribution to the outside of the circle. Approximately twice as much water falls at the 1½-foot mark as at 7½ feet.

The three sprinklers that made this pattern were:

(1) One of the familiar fixed round heads that throws a circle (or segment of a circle) of misty spray. This is the type that is used extensively in permanent underground sprinkler systems.

(2) A sprinkler with a rapidly whirling baffle on top that directs the spray in a square shape.

(3) A traveling sprinkler, operated by an internal water-driven motor, winds up a tethered tape in order to creep. It has a rapidly whirling spray arm.

This pattern can be very useful, but you must operate it knowingly. If you are careful to overlap your patterns as much as is necessary, you will get an even water penetration. This is what takes place when sprinkler number

one in this group is used in a well-designed, many-head, underground system. The overlap of many such sprinklers compensates for the single head's uneven penetration pattern.

Suppose you were to set a sprinkler like this in the same spots down the middle of a rectangular lawn each week. From the spray pattern you see in the air, you would judge that you were covering the entire rectangle and doing right by your grass. Actually, you would be putting from one to two inches in the middle of the apparently wetted area, and only a trace of water near the outer edges. The answer, of course, is to set your sprinklers in successive overlapping positions. To establish overlap, make the coffee can test described on page 25 There is only one special problem in using the fixed round head type of sprinkler: when the wind blows hard, it picks up the mist and blows it away, making for lopsided water dispersal. Try to use this sprinkler type in still air.

For about the first 6 feet from the center, our traveling sprinkler gave quite even coverage. As a rule, sprinklers with water-driven internal parts, such as this traveler, seem to put out somewhat less water per minute than the simpler devices at the same pressure.

If you overlap either of the first two sprinklers on this list to make an even pattern, you either wet the sidewalk or give less water to the outside edges of the lawn. If you have a traveling sprinkler that makes the kind of pattern ours did, increase the diameter setting to overlap the lawn edges a little. Then the edges won't suffer.

PATTERN B. Single round head sprinkler is the type that is used extensively in permanent underground systems. Amount of water diminishes fast toward edges of wetted area, but pattern is a good one if overlapped

PATTERN C. Slowly revolving sprinkler is a classic among portable lawn sprinklers. It has propelling jets at ends of arm, makes a spiral spray pattern in air

Wetting Pattern C:
Useful But Erratic . . . Very Common

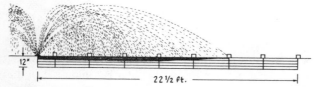

FOUR SPRINKLERS tested made this pattern, varying in degree. Most of the water falls from 4 to 8 feet out

Pattern C—Heavy on the inside but even heavier four to seven feet from the sprinkler, gradually diminishing to the edge.

The four sprinklers that made this kind of pattern in our tests (varying in degree, mostly depending on the volume of water delivered) were:

(1) A sprinkler that looks the same as number 1 in pattern B, but instead of making a mist spray out of its round head, a sleeve pops up and delivers the spray in fast droplets.

(2) The long plastic hose or tube in which water sprays through many fine holes.

(3) The old classic lawn sprinkler that revolves slowly—with propelling jets at the end of the arms to make a spiral spray pattern in the air. It is pictured in operation in the photograph above.

(4) Another old classic, the sprinkler in which water

squirts out of many sieve holes.

If one of these sprinklers throws water out wide enough to wet the entire width of your lawn, the slightly erratic pattern will hardly be worth worrying about. You can overlap patterns slightly, but you can never correct the fact that more water drops at 4½ feet than at 1½ feet. Sprinklers that make a severe version of this pattern are grouped under pattern D (they have more serious shortcomings).

Sprinkler number 1 in this pattern is often used in permanent underground systems. There, its slightly erratic pattern is more than offset by an advantage: The water shoots out in large drops, so there is little or no mist for the wind to blow around. The water is distributed more evenly than a misty spray from a fixed head. All the fixed round sprinkler heads are also available in forms that make a half or quarter circle to fit corners or sides, thereby making it possible to soak a lawn evenly and not wet the sidewalk. With just one full round head on a portable sprinkler, you would have to wet the sidewalk in order to put enough water along the edges.

The long plastic hose or tube with small holes in it comes in many different models. You can lay such a tube down the middle of a small rectangular lawn (perhaps edging it into the wind if it blows across the lawn) and, standing at the faucet, adjust the water volume until you just exactly cover the rectangle. Better let a little go over the edges because at 16½ feet in our tests the cups received just a trace of water.

This is one characteristic you should allow for with some types of plastic tube sprinklers: Holes closest to the faucet may put out more water than those at the other end because of friction loss inside the tube. If you are a perfectionist, the answer would be to switch the direction of a tube with this kind of delivery end-for-end when you are halfway through the watering.

The whirling sprinkler we tested delivered a fairly even water pattern, but there are so many versions of this type that we can't say that our pattern is representative. You can't water a lawn evenly with our model and avoid overlapping the edge.

Sieve-type sprinklers are made in a number of different shapes. In some the fine holes are arranged around a ring. In others the holes are in a central inverted cup. The one we used was of the latter type. Other forms make somewhat different wetting patterns. In our test no water went beyond 16½ feet. But up through 13½ feet, the dispersal was remarkably even. This kind of pattern would call for overlapping just the outer 3 feet of each spray pattern.

Pattern D: Wide, Cone-Shaped . . .

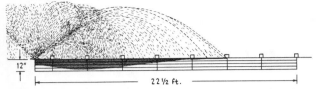

HERE IS the kind of soaking that results. Growth would be uneven if you always watered in the same place

Pattern D—The greatest amount of sprinkler water falls about halfway out on the radius line of the apparently wetted area.

"Old Owl-Eyes" made this pattern. This little old-timer (you can hold it on the palm of your hand) sends water through two big holes that look like owl's eyes. It makes a wide, cone-shaped spray.

If you were to water your lawn with this sprinkler, or any that make a pattern like it, in the same spots each week, you would end up in trouble unless you have a soil that drains ideally. Overlapping by itself will not make this kind of pattern even. Best thing you can do, come watering day, is to run your sprinkler at half-pressure, and move it to as many different positions on the lawn as

PATTERN D. This may look like even dispersal, but it isn't. Almost twice as much water was caught in the second cup as in the cup nearest the sprinkler head

you can. "Old Owl-Eyes" does a useful job in borders and plant beds where it acts not so much as a sprinkler but as a gentle water dispenser for flood-irrigating.

A sprinkler like this, run at half-pressure, would serve well for localized, long, slow soaks on a lawn. Sometimes slow soaks alone will make hard spots take water once again as they should. Canvas tube soakers will do the same thing.

Pattern E: The Fan Spray . . .

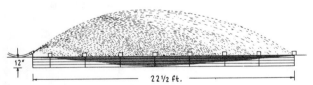

MEASURE IT and you will see that it puts most of the water between 7 and 14 feet from the sprinkler head

Pattern E—An extremely heavy catch of water out at 6 to 12 feet, with practically no water dropping in by the sprinkler.

The only one of our sprinklers that made this extreme pattern was the nailhead spike type, which sprays water through a slit in its head into a fan that covers about a 90° arc.

In the tests, this well-known device looked for all the world as though it were spraying evenly all over the area the water covered. But it didn't. We could have done almost as well by running a hose directly onto the lawn at a position 13½ feet from the sprinkler. This

wetting pattern is useful for watering shrubbery or odd corners in a lawn. You also could put it to use in a long, narrow lawn by moving it each time to the exact spot that got the water from the previous setting.

On a calm day you can do some useful tricks with this sprinkler. Tilt it back a little and the water will cover a neat little ellipse, close to the spike. Tilt it farther and it will make a vertical sheet of water that falls in a straight line.

PATTERN E. The nailhead sprinkler leaves an extremely heavy catch of water 6 to 12 feet out, but very little water drops in the area close to the sprinkler

Installing a Sprinkler System

Since publication of the last edition of this book there has been one significant change in underground sprinkler systems. Probably 90 per cent of all pipe and fittings used today, both commercially and for home installation, is plastic rather than metallic. Galvanized iron pipe (the most popular material a little over ten years ago) and copper tubing are still used, mostly for very large installations and in communities where plastic materials have not won full code approval.

Today, you can choose from several time-tested plastic systems. These offer the homeowner advantages in cost, ease of installation, and speed of installation (by the homeowner). If he puts in his own plastic or non-metallic system, the homeowner can usually do the job for less than half the cost of a galvanized iron sprinkler system, professionally installed, and he can complete an installation for the average size residential lawn in a day or so. Non-metallic installations are either semi-rigid or flexible plastic pipe.

Non-metallic pipe and fittings have been widely used in typical residential sprinkling systems for many years; and pipe made from similar materials has been used satisfactorily underground for much longer in commercial installations. The pipe materials do appear to solve many problems inherent in burying any pipe underground. Plastic fittings are similar in appearance to the metal fittings, differing only in material and method of joining.

There are five advantages to non-metallic systems:

1. They are very easy to install. The homeowner can complete an average residential installation in one day.

2. They can be tested above ground before final installation. This is particularly important when the inexperienced homeowner does the work himself. He can test the sprinkling pattern for complete coverage by means of the coffee can test described on page 25, move the pipe as necessary, then bury it underground.

3. There is minimum disturbance of existing lawn or garden during installation. With an all-metal system, you must dig a trench for room to work with pipe wrenches, or a torch in the case of copper, whereas a space slit in the lawn is usually all that is needed in order to bury the new flexible or semi-rigid pipe. The lawn can then be tamped back in place in a few minutes' time.

4. Non-metallic pipe material is not affected by corrosion, rust, or electrolysis. This means that it should last as long or longer than galvanized iron pipe when buried underground, and efficiency within the system will not change significantly as it gets older.

5. Plastic pipe has less friction loss per foot, thus a pipe of a given size will carry more water than the same size galvanized iron pipe. The rate of flow for plastic is about the same as for copper.

COSTS

Costs for all sprinkler systems vary, but you can figure on paying 6 to 9 cents per square foot (lawn area) for materials to install plastic systems. A plastic system with metal risers and heads can be obtained for slightly less cost than a galvanized system. It is easier to install, however, than the galvanized. Materials alone for the galvanized iron system may run more than 14 cents per square foot for a satisfactory coverage. Fully installed (by a professional) and guaranteed, the all-metal system will cost as much as 18 to 25 cents per square foot.

DURABILITY AND SERVICE

Since plastic pipe material cannot be affected by electrolysis, rust, or corrosion, it should not build up interior deposits impairing flow efficiency. Nor should pipe material rust and deteriorate from the outside.

There seems to be no absolute guarantee that rodents won't attack either new pipe material. Rodent damage to plastic pipes has been reported in eastern parts of Washington. But, on the other hand, five million feet of cellulose acetate butyrate type of plastic pipe material (similar to that now available for home use) have been installed by one Southern California utility company over the past 15 years, with no reports of gopher problems. Manufacturers of PVC plastic pipe say that their material is so hard and smooth that rodents cannot get a tooth-hold on this pipe.

The most common cause of damage reported is from digging into the pipe with a spade or other garden tool. This can be avoided by burying the lateral lines at least six inches below the surface. At this depth the pipe should also be safe from the tines of an aerating tool. However, if damaged, plastic pipe can be repaired much more easily than metal pipe. Simply dig a small hole at the trouble spot, cut out the damaged section, and cement or clamp in a new coupling section.

Here are several warnings on the non-metallic sprinkler systems:

Water pressures exceeding 60 pounds per square inch may force open the joints or rupture some plastic pipe. You may avoid this by installation of a pressure regulator valve, or by using a plastic pipe rated for an operating pressure of 100 pounds per square inch or more. This need not be a serious problem, however, for an operating sprinkler system is constantly bleeding-off pressure. You could use high-test pipe (Class 315 PVC pipe has been approved by some communities for service from the water meter to house), from control valves to the first two or three heads, and regular weight pipe from that point on, for each circuit.

Deal with an established nursery, garden supply store, plumber, or installer when buying pipe materials and fittings. Make sure that the company manufacturing the pipe will definitely stand behind its product and will guarantee it against material defects. Some systems are guaranteed up to 20 years.

If you live in a region where the ground freezes in winter, check with your dealer or manufacturer before investing in a plastic system; and in any system, install a drain valve.

If you live in an area of extreme heat, remember that most plastic pipe is rated for an operating temperature of 73° Fahrenheit. If your water temperature exceeds that, check with the manufacturer before using plastic pipe.

As with any project you undertake, the quality of the final product will depend largely upon how well it was planned, how closely the plans were followed, and the quality of workmanship.

USING A PLANNING SERVICE

You can usually get advice on installation of a sprinkler system from your garden or plumbing supply dealer. In addition, many manufacturers of home sprinkler equipment have a planning service, and will provide you with complete specifications for installation, including a list of parts needed. Sometimes a small charge is made for this service, but often it is available without additional cost when you buy your materials.

To use this service you would have to provide the designer with the following information:

1. The area to be irrigated. This should be furnished in the form of an accurate sketch, drawn to scale, showing buildings, walks, trees, shrubbery, or any other obstacles which may affect the plan. Also, mention slope if it is significant. Be sure to mark the area you want covered by the sprinkler system.

2. Determine the static water pressure. Your local water company can give you a figure for this, but it is better to borrow a pressure gauge from your dealer or water company and check the pressure several times during different days to find the *minimum* pressure under which your system will have to operate.

3. The size of the meter. This is usually $3/4$ inch or 1 inch. If it is a $1/2$ inch meter, you may have to ask your water company to install one of larger size.

4. The size and length of the main service line (from the meter to the house). Be sure to say whether this line is galvanized iron or copper pipe, and state approximately how old it is.

If you can, also mention the number and type of valves, fittings, and couplings the water will flow through before it reaches the point where you intend to cut into the main service line.

From this information the designer will be able to calculate the theoretical volume of water and pressure available to operate your sprinkling system. He can then divide the area into separate circuits which will operate most efficiently on the water available, taking into consideration loss of pressure and flow due to friction.

DESIGNING YOUR OWN SPRINKLING SYSTEM

If you decide to design your own sprinkling system, here are some of the basic rules to follow.

1. Determine the available water volume and pressure. You can find the pressure with a gauge in the same manner as outlined above. To find the volume you might first measure the flow from an open pipe near the point where you plan to cut into the main service line. This could be done by turning off the main control valve and then removing a hose bib valve so that you could obtain full flow from the pipe. You could then open the main control valve and time the flow of one cubic foot of water through your meter. (On the face of your meter you will find one dial marked "one foot." One complete revolution of the hand on this dial indicates one cubic foot of flow.)

If this took 25 seconds, you could figure on .04 cubic feet of water per second, or 2.40 cubic feet of water per minute. As the rate of discharge of sprinkler heads is usually stated in gallons per minute, convert this to gallons by multiplying by 7.48, for a total of 17.95 gallons per minute as the total amount of water available at the point where your system will start.

2. Next, make a drawing of the area to be watered. You can do this easily with only a pencil and ruler by using graph paper. You will also need a compass to draw sprinkler coverages. Draw in buildings, trees, and any other obstacles.

3. Tentatively select the sprinklers most satisfactory for your situation. Consider size of area, rate of discharge of the heads, and rate of precipitation. (If your soil is heavy clay and water penetration is slow, you will probably want a sprinkler head which will apply water slowly.) Also, consider the pressure necessary to operate the heads you choose.

4. With a compass, draw to scale the coverage of each sprinkler. You can use either triangular or square spacing, according to your lot plan. Triangular spacing requires fewer heads to cover a given area. Lap sprinkler coverage about 60%, or more if you have a wind problem, to equalize distribution of water and to make sure every part of the lawn will be adequately irrigated. Try several different layouts to find the best pattern for your particular area.

5. After you have chosen the heads you will use, total the number of gallons discharged per minute for each head and compare this sum with the volume of water available. In this way you can decide how many circuits you will need, and, by computing friction loss, whether you will have enough pressure to operate that number of heads. Be sure to allow a margin of reserve for variations in pressure. Total pressure loss due to friction is determined by size, length, and condition of pipe. Use the table on page 35 to estimate this pressure loss.

6. Determine the most convenient location for your operating valves. Be sure to choose a place where you can turn the water on and off without getting wet. In most cases this will probably be close to your existing hose bib. If shrubbery or planting beds surround the hose bib, or you find that it will be within range of the sprinkler pattern, install your operating valves somewhere more convenient.

CHOICE OF SPRINKLER HEADS

With the variety of sprinkler heads available today you have a wide choice of possible systems. Different heads vary in volume and pressure requirements from approxi-

mately .5 gallons per minute delivery at about 10 pounds pressure for a quarter head with an 8-foot radius pattern, to about 10 gallons per minute at 30 pounds pressure with a coverage diameter of 50 feet. These figures are optimum for certain plan heads and special high capacity "pop-up" heads. Some of the latter will throw a rectangular pattern, one 5 by 25 feet, and another 5 by 40 feet. These are designed for parkways and other narrow strips. Others have square patterns from 18 by 18 to 30 by 30 feet. However, none of the sprinklers we have tested has uniform precipitation over the entire area of coverage. Unless your soil has excellent drainage characteristics, we recommend that you plan an overlapping layout rather than try to cover the entire area with one high-capacity head.

Rotating "impulse" type sprinklers operate at from 20 to 80 pounds pressure, discharging from about 2 to 36 gallons of water per minute. Throwing radii for these sprinklers range from 22 to 77 feet. These are ideal for larger areas where wind is not a serious problem — the trajectory height of the stream from these sprinklers is from 3 to 6 feet, depending on nozzle angle and pressure.

The plain and "pop-up" sprinklers are set flush with the ground level, while the "impulse" type must be installed above ground level. These, however, can be installed with self-closing flush valves and keys which allow simple removal of the heads when not in use, and also permit each head to be used on several different circuits.

Patterns and coverage for heads vary, but correspond closely to patterns discussed under portable sprinklers. The "impulse" type has a pattern similar to pattern A, the plain head similar to pattern B, and the "pop-up" head similar to pattern C.

Most sprinkler systems use only one type of head, with quarter and half heads along walks and other places as needed. It is possible, however, to use different heads in one system if you use only heads of the same precipitation rate on one circuit. Heads of different precipitation rates can be used on different circuits, and the same total precipitation can be realized by varying the length of time each circuit is turned on. Some manufacturers give the precipitation rate for their sprinklers; and for those who don't, here is one way you can determine it: multiply the rate of discharge in gallons per minute by the conversion factor 96.3, and then divide this by the product of the distance between heads on a line and the distance between lines.

Some sprinkler heads operate efficiently over a wide pressure range, with an increase of pressure increasing the diameter of the pattern. Others are made to operate effectively only in a more narrow range of ten pounds more or less than the pressure specified. These heads usually have a constant throw diameter. In plotting this latter type of head in your layout, use a constant size circle, and use a sufficient number of heads on each circuit to reduce the pressure to recommended operating levels. If the length of pipe or the number of heads used is not sufficient to reduce pressure to that recommended, it would be advisable to install a pressure regulator.

CONTROL OF PRESSURE

Control of pressure can be partially achieved for impulse heads by the size and length of the pipe used. If it is necessary to reduce the radius of a "pop-up" sprinkler head, a restrictor can be used in the risers. Some plain heads have an adjustable built-in restrictor.

Ideal pressure (that for which most sprinkling systems have been designed) is from 40 to 60 pounds per square inch. If your pressure is below 30 pounds, chances are that any sprinkling system will be not only expensive, but usually ineffective in its coverage unless you have large main service pipes and can install large size laterals in your system. Also, low pressure can be overcome by installing a booster pump. Some sprinkler heads have been designed to operate at low pressures, provided flow is sufficient. One impulse head will cover a 27-foot circle at five pounds pressure, using 1.89 gallons of water per minute. If it is over 60 pounds, the high pressure may affect the spray pattern and tend to cause the water to fog.

You can estimate the pressure drop in your sprinkler system from the table below, which indicates the loss of pressure for each 10 feet of pipe for ½ and ¾-inch and 1-inch pipe. These figures are approximate for galvanized iron and plastic pipe. Approximate pressure loss in flow of water through 10 feet of pipe:

Pipe size	5 g.p.m.	10 g.p.m.	15 g.p.m.	20 g.p.m.
½ inch GI	2.0	6.5	15.5	....
Plastic	1.7	5.7	11.1	....
¾ inch GI	.5	1.5	3.5	6.0
Plastic	.4	1.1	2.7	4.5
1 inch GI	.1	.5	1.0	2.0
Plastic	.1	.4	.75	1.5

(Note: In old, corroded iron pipe, flow may be reduced by up to 50%.)

Polyethylene pipe with insert fittings is rated about the same as galvanized iron pipe of the same size. Manufacturers of PVC pipe state one size smaller than iron pipe will provide approximately the same flow. This is partially due to the improved fittings.

Another way you can determine the number of heads to use per line or on each circuit is by pressure and pipe size:

(Based on ¾-inch main not over 50 feet in length)

Type of head	Shower				Pop-up				Impulse			
Pressure	30	40	50	60	30	40	50	60	30	40	50	60
Number of heads on ½-inch lateral	3	4	4	5	2	2	3	4		1	1	1
¾-inch lateral	4	6	7	8	2	4	5	6	1	1	3	3

(In computing heads per line, figure ½ circle heads at ⅔ full circle delivery, ¼ heads at ⅓ delivery.)

If you live in a neighborhood where new houses are likely to be built, make allowance for some drop in water pressure which may take place as neighborhood water consumption increases.

Plans on the following two pages show different methods of locating heads on a typical front lawn. Each method should provide adequate coverage. Materials for the system shown in Figure A would cost about $20 to $35 more than those for the system shown in Figure B, but would provide more even coverage, waste less water on street and driveway, and probably cost less in the long run.

Let's assume that you find your water pressure to be about 45 pounds at your hose bib. By using the previous table, figuring conservatively at 40 pounds, you'll find that ¾-inch pipe will serve 6 plain sprinkler heads on any one line. Therefore, 3 lines could serve either layout shown in Figure A and Figure B. (Almost all installers recommend using ¾-inch pipe throughout the system, except on terminal sections of a branch line system. See Figure D on next page.)

The pattern in which the pipe is laid out is not too important except that a pressure drop occurs with every elbow, Tee, or fitting in the line. By laying out your system with the fewest fittings and the shortest runs of pipe possible, you will get the most efficient and economical sprinkling system.

In some locations where there is a strong prevailing wind, installers often try to take the wind into consideration when laying out the plan. This can be done beforehand on top of the ground with either the plastic or rubber systems.

Where the sprinkler system connects to house main or hose bib, you will need a control valve for each line.

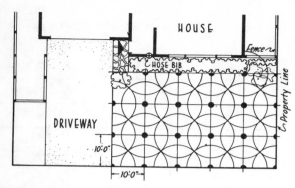

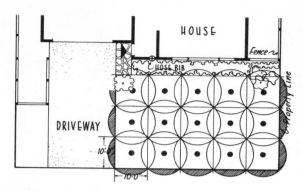

FIGURE A. To obtain complete coverage with no waste, layout above used eight full circle heads, eleven 1/2 circle heads, one 3/4 circle head, three 1/4 circle heads

FIGURE B. Layout was made with 14 full circle heads, one 3/4 circle head. System would give complete coverage, but it would waste some water around the edges

Most communities require an anti-siphon valve which guarantees against back siphoning of surface water into the service main. Some communities require an anti-siphon control valve for each circuit and specify that valves should be installed 6 or 7 inches above ground. Always check local regulations before buying valves.

Selection of valves is also important in preventing loss of pressure. A fully opened globe valve has the same effect on loss of pressure as about 20 feet of pipe of the same size. An angle valve, as shown in the drawing below at right, effects pressure only half as much, and a gate valve has less resistance to flow than a standard Tee.

AT LEFT: Connection of system with an anti-siphon control valve above ground. AT RIGHT: Three-line system has control valves, operated with special key, in sleeves below the ground. Note the anti-siphon valve

If your system takes off directly from the existing hose bib, the amount of water available will be limited to the hose bib. Thus, if the hose bib is 3/4-inch pipe, you will be able to run only one 3/4-inch line of the system at any one time. To make more water available, you can cut into the supply line to your house if it is larger. This can be made by cutting out a short section of line, threading

both ends, and placing a Tee fitting onto the line. Complete the connection with a nipple and union.

Another method of cutting into a line is with a special slip-joint Tee. Cut out one inch of the existing steel line, slip on the Tee, and tighten each end with a small pipe wrench. If you are not experienced in working with pipe, have this job done by a professional.

If you are installing the system in your back yard, it is better to extend your main service line and by-pass the house than to cut into any of the lines serving the house. If you have a pressure regulator, by-pass it to assure maximum pressure for your sprinklers.

If you live in a region where the ground freezes in winter, don't forget to provide a drain sump into which you can drain the entire system before frost. Check with your hardware dealer or sprinkler contractor for local practices.

INSTALLATION OF A SPRINKLING SYSTEM

We recommend that you read through these general instructions for installing each type of system before you choose the one you want to install yourself. Whatever system you install, we also recommend that the line from your water main to the control valves be either copper or galvanized iron, whichever the main line is.

Plastic

The systems now on the market fall into two different classifications; semi-rigid pipe and flexible pipe. Some installers who have worked with the flexible plastic pipe claim that it is more difficult to install than the semi-rigid pipe. Plastic pipe is more easily installed in warm weather than in cold, because the pipe is more flexible. Some manufacturers suggest metal risers; in the case of

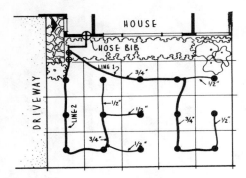

FIGURE C. Pipe layout shown above uses the snake pattern most easily adapted to flexible pipe. You can lay out any pattern, running around any obstacles

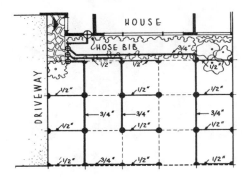

FIGURE D. Layout with branch line pattern works with any type pipe. The system was designed for three lines because of pressure drop due to the numerous fittings

impulse heads, unless metal risers are used, the riser should be cemented or strapped to a firm metal stake to prevent it from vibrating loose. Risers normally sold with plastic systems are ½-inch or ¾-inch rigid plastic, 4 inches in length.

The simplified directions which follow refer to the types of pipe now on the market. Though both ABS and PVC pipe are called "semi-rigid," ABS is actually flexible enough to be laid in a curve with a minimum five-foot radius.

The semi-rigid plastic pipe is available in varying lengths from 5 to 20 feet. Longer or shorter lengths can be assembled easily by cutting with a hacksaw and joining sections with couplings. Flexible plastic pipe can be bought in lengths from 200 to 1000 feet. On ABS and PVC pipe, plastic-to-plastic joints are secured with a cement compound which, in effect, welds pipe and fitting into one permanently joined piece. Polyethylene pipe fittings are inserted into the flexible pipe and secured with metal clamps. One manufacturer has developed "full flow" fittings to use with special ⅞-inch polyethylene pipe. They require no cement or special tools.

The Tee's and Ell's of plastic systems are threaded to take standard ½-inch or ¾-inch pipe or rigid plastic risers. This makes it possible to install longer temporary risers for new lawn, or use longer risers if the ground level raises, as it often does on lawns after a period of years.

To install a plastic pipe system, first determine the location of each sprinkler head and drive a stake in the ground. Lay out your plastic pipe and metal or plastic fittings on top of the ground to conform to the pattern and set-up on paper. When you are satisfied that you have all materials on hand for the complete installation,

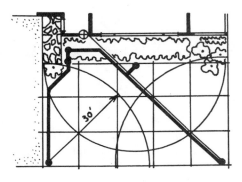

FIGURE E. Three "impulse" heads set for semi-circular coverage. This layout uses considerably less pipe and fewer fittings than any of the other four examples

begin joining the pipe and fittings.

With flexible plastic pipe, uncoil from the control valve out, following the pattern previously laid out in your plan. Cut the pipe at each point where a fitting is needed, and clamp the fitting to the pipe.

The great advantage of plastic pipe is the complete flexibility. You can lay out any pattern, running the pipe around trees, shrubs, or any other obstacle without installing 90° angle fittings which lower the pipe's efficiency.

When the complete pipe line has been laid out, insert risers into the Tee's and tie them to the stakes for temporary support. Join the pipe line to the water main and valve. If you used semi-rigid plastic pipe, allow at least an hour for the cement to dry thoroughly. Then turn on the water and flush out the entire pipe system. Install the heads and turn the water on again to check the coverage. If any change in the layout is required to effect more

FLEXIBLE PIPE INSTALLATION. Installation of plastic or rubber sprinkling system is simple matter once the plan has been determined. Trial layout is staked out above ground, ready for testing to see if sprinkler pattern gives desired coverage. Layout can easily be altered if necessary to rectify any planning errors

even coverage, you can easily move the stake and head or insert restrictors.

Allow the sprinkler system to soak the sod thoroughly; then cut a "V" or slit in the sod along the pipe line. If the turf is soft enough, you can accomplish this satisfactorily by inserting the spade into the ground, then rocking it back and forth until you have opened a slot deep enough for the pipe.

PLASTIC. Semi-rigid plastic cuts easily with hacksaw. Plastic-to-plastic joints are secured with a cement compound which welds pipe and fitting into one piece

In some soils you may have to dig a small trench in order to place the pipe deep enough for the risers you use. In any event, it is advisable to place the pipe below the level reached by lawn aerators.

Bury the system to the proper depth so that the heads are flush with the established sod; then tamp the sod back in place. A heavy steel tamper helps with this job. On a new lawn, follow the same procedure as described for galvanized iron systems.

Galvanized Iron

You can usually buy materials from plumbers or pipe yards. Also, look in the section headed "Sprinklers—Lawn & Irrigation" in the yellow pages of your phone book to find who carries complete sprinkler system supplies. Since prices for pipe and fittings often vary, it may pay you to consult more than one source.

Unless you are especially energetic, have the pipe cut and threaded to lengths specified in your plan, rather than try to do the job yourself. The cost differential is rarely worth the labor involved when an unskilled homeowner tackles the job of cutting and threading pipe.

Buy the necessary pipe valves, unions, fittings, and lay out the line on top of the ground, to make sure you have all the required pieces.

If you are installing the system in a new lawn, sprinkler heads should be installed on temporary risers which extend above the level of the ground. When the lawn is established and the soil has finally settled, you can install new risers which will bring the heads flush with the

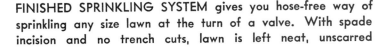

SPADE MAKES INCISION for flexible pipe. The new pipe materials can be installed with very little disturbance of existing lawn area

FINISHED SPRINKLING SYSTEM gives you hose-free way of sprinkling any size lawn at the turn of a valve. With spade incision and no trench cuts, lawn is left neat, unscarred

surface of the sod. Normally, you will be able to borrow temporary risers where you buy your pipe and fittings.

On established lawns, you will need to dig a trench from 4 to 12 inches wide and 6 to 8 inches deep. This can be done with a small, portable power trenching machine which can be rented at some supply stores. Fittings are made with a pipe wrench in place, then the soil is filled in and the sod replaced on top. Sprinkler heads should be

installed flush with the lawn surface.

Be sure to run a full head of water through the system to blow out any soil or foreign material from the pipe and fittings before you finally screw on the heads.

Pipe joints should be sealed with white lead or a pipe joint compound as this will help retard rust and corrosion at the threads where the galvanizing has been scraped

GALVANIZED IRON. Most installers recommend that the pipe be laid 6 to 8 inches below the surface. Note the two pipe wrenches that are used to adjust joints

ALL-METAL INSTALLATION on existing lawn. You will need to dig a trench about 12 inches wide. Sod is then replaced on top after installation is completed

away. It is also a good idea to paint any marks made by the jaws of your pipe wrenches. Always work from the control valves out toward the end of the line as you are installing any sprinkler system.

AUTOMATION IN WATERING

When you plan your sprinkling system, you might want to consider the advantages of automatic irrigation control.

Golf courses, parks, schools, and industries with large areas to irrigate have been using automatic watering controls for years. Manufacturers have now scaled equipment down for use in home sprinkling systems.

There are three main components in any automatic sprinkler control:

1. The timer. This is an electric clock mechanism which drives a dial or other indicator upon which the watering schedule is pre-set. (There are also wind-up models for areas where electricity is not readily available.)

2. The valves. These are opened and closed by hydraulic pressure. They can be remotely located, near the circuit they control, or located in the same positions as valves manually operated. An advantage to remote location is the possible saving in length of pipe used. This can amount to savings in cost of pipe.

3. Connection between timer and valves. Timers are used to actuate the valves by three different methods. In each method, the valves are operated by differential hydraulic pressure.

One type of connection is mechanical. The movement of a lever or switch exposes a chamber in the valve to hydraulic pressure so that it opens or closes.

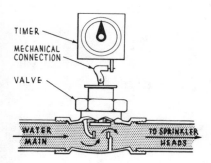

SINGLE VALVE CONTROLLER has timer mounted above valve. Mechanical movement actuates valve

Another type of control is by a solenoid (an electromagnetic switch) connected to the timer at the control box. The action of the solenoid opens or closes a valve on a small copper or plastic tube connecting the main

water line with the control valve, thus supplying or relieving hydraulic pressure.

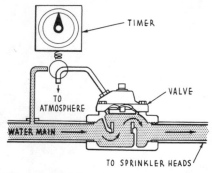

SOLENOID mounted in control box at house actuates valve by hydraulic pressure through buried tubing

A third type of control has a solenoid located at the control valve and is connected to the timer by underground wiring. It is called an electric valve.

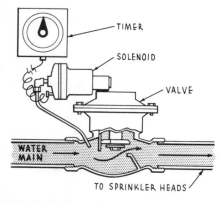

ELECTRIC WIRE runs underground from timer on house wall to the solenoid mounted directly on the valve

Remote control valves are designed in either a normally closed or normally open position. "Normally closed" means that the valve, under the pressure of the water main only, is closed. Pressure is applied by the action of the control mechanism to open the valve for sprinkling. In the "normally open" valve, pressure is applied through the control line to close the valve, and the solenoid acts to bleed off pressure at sprinkling time.

Each type has its particular advantages. In the event of electric power failure, or a broken pressure line, the "normally closed" valve will remain closed. You need not worry about a flooded lawn or basement. On the other hand, a broken pressure line may go unnoticed when sprinkling is scheduled at night, until the unwatered section attracts attention.

With the "normally open" valve system, you will know immediately when a break occurs, since the damaged section will sprinkle continuously. Some models using this type of valve include an automatic device to close the valves if the power fails.

Worth checking is whether, in case of power failure, the controller will resume its scheduled operation automatically when the power comes on again. Some models must be re-started by hand. For the absent owner, this might mean a badly parched or flooded garden.

Kits to fit valves of existing sprinkling systems are also available for simple conversion to automatic watering.

Use of automatic irrigation

Here are some of the possible situations where automatic controls might be used to advantage.

If you have a problem with water running off because of slope or slow penetration, you can cycle the system so that it will water for short periods of time between certain hours on one or two days each week.

If different parts of your lawn have different rates of penetration, or different grade, you could cycle different circuits for different time periods so that each part of the lawn would get only the water it needed, and one part would not be soaked while another was only partially watered.

If you were just starting to landscape your yard, you could plan for eventual complete automatic watering for the entire yard, using special sprinkler heads for shrubs and trees. By using a large multi-station controller (one model will control from 5 to 33 valves), you can plan for expansion if you have a large lot which you are developing by stages.

Watering can be done automatically at night or during the early morning hours, leaving the lawn unsoaked and free for use during the evening hours.

Timing can be cycled for frequent, brief periods for new lawns, or can be altered according to the time of year and rate of soil water loss due to temperature and wind changes.

Automatic controls can have their watering cycle manually by-passed during rainy weather, and some systems have devices which automatically keep the valves closed when nature takes over the watering duties.

Other optional equipment includes skip-timing wheels for odd or even day watering, switching circuits to start and stop supply pumps, and moisture indicators which actuate the controller when soil moisture drops below a predetermined point.

Two types of indicators are used to determine soil moisture for regulation of automatic controllers. One, called a hydrostat, works on a vacuum principle. A porous porcelain-tipped tube containing water is buried at root depth. When the soil dries out, it absorbs the water from the tube through the porcelain, creating a vacuum in the tube. The other type of indicator is a pair of low-voltage electric probes buried parallel to each other, measuring the electrical resistance of the soil between them. The controller opens the valves in the system at a pre-set time of day after the indicator signals that the soil moisture is low. The timer will repeat its cycle, according to its setting, until the indicator signals that ground moisture is again sufficient.

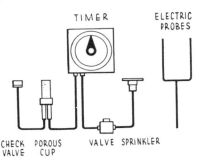

MOISTURE INDICATORS: Left, porous vacuum cup actuates timer. Right, probes actuate timer electrically

Obviously, the range of automatic features is extensive. You can probably find the right combination of features to meet your watering needs best in one of the many models now available. What a control costs depends largely on the amount of automation, and the number of valves (one for each sprinkler circuit) the system requires. Valves range in price from $6 (for one-inch pipe) to $39, and in materials from high-impact plastic to solid brass. Equipment, including timer, for a one-valve system would cost between $75 and $100. Larger units may run as high as $1000. Initial cost may be partially off-set by savings in pipe and water.

Installation precautions

If you decide to install a controller yourself, check with your local building inspector's office. Improper electric wiring can be dangerous, especially around water. Codes vary, and in some places any underground wiring must be encased with rigid metal conduit. Also, many plumbing codes require anti-siphon valves to prevent back-siphonage which might contaminate the house water supply.

You may need a permit, and the inspector will check your work before it is buried. Bury underground wiring 14 to 18 inches deep to avoid damage when gardening.

Lawn Mowing and Grooming

The grass must be cut—no question about that. But with what? How high? Leave the clippings or not? What else must you do to make the lawn neat and blemish-free? Should you hire out your lawn mowing to a professional gardener or to a small boy in the neighborhood, or should you do it yourself?

There just are no pat answers to these questions.

Different grasses require different upkeep. Home owners have different ideas about what a well-groomed lawn should look like. Manufacturers of lawn mowers and lawn edgers offer different models that do the job in different ways, cut in different widths, have different horsepowers, different engine types. Some people like engines and will have power tools no matter what. Others like the sound and the exercise of pushing a hand mower.

Lawns, being the individual little plant communities that they are, respond in different ways to clippings or no clippings, high cuttings or low cuttings.

We certainly will make no recommendation here on the ideal combination of machinery and methods for grooming a lawn. But we will report the observations we have made and what *Sunset* readers have reported to us.

From left to right in the large photograph, you see a hand-operated reel mower, a power reel mower, a power rotary mower. These are your three principal choices in lawn mowing machinery. There are a few other basic kinds of mowers, but they are designed for commercial use and seem to be priced too high for home use.

THE HAND-OPERATED REEL MOWER

For many years, this machine alone was a lawn mower to most people. Today, on a small lawn, a well-built, well-maintained, hand-operated reel mower can still hold its own against its power-driven brethren.

If your total lawn area is less than 2,000 square feet, time saving is not the real argument for a power rig. When you consider the time it takes to get the bulkier power machine out of storage, check the fuel, tend to its engine needs, mow the lawn, and then clean it before you put it away, you probably come out about the same in amount of time consumed.

But in energy consumed, it's a different matter. No doubt about it, out on the lawn the little 1 to 4-hp engine does take the place of your legs and back.

If you like exercise, and if you think your garden should be a place of peace and quiet, the hand machine may still be your best answer. Only an electric-powered rotary mower is quieter. If you keep the bearings oiled on a hand mower, and if you get it sharpened every year and keep it adjusted, it will remain a comparatively quiet machine and will serve you for years. (A perfectly adjusted reel mower will cut a piece of paper between reel blade and the bed knife.) The hand mower scores high on portability and easy storage. You can brace it against a wall or hang it on the studs. A 16-inch hand model requires only 9 cubic feet of storage area (2 feet by 1 foot by 4½ feet).

Low price, of course, is the other basic advantage of the hand mower. Most hand mower models cost just a little more than half the price of a typically priced rotary mower.

THE REEL-MOWING PRINCIPLE

Any reel mower, hand or power-driven, makes a comparatively smooth and even cut. You get neat little crosswise marks and a "striped" effect on the over-all lawn. (Loose reel bearings or dull blades may emphasize this.)

To mow bent or Bermuda grass, both of which thrive on very close mowing, you can set most reel mowers as low as ½ inch. (The inexpensive rotary mowers won't go that low.)

The typical reel mower has 5 blades, although some economy models have 4. There is a trend to 6 and 7 blade models for cutting low or wiry grass, such as Bermuda and bent. Putting green mowers have up to 12 blades. In Bermuda grass country (Los Angeles, for instance) professional gardeners demand a very low cutting, 6 or 7-blade rotary, and manufacturers make such

HAND REEL
12" to 19" cut

GASOLINE REEL
16" to 24" cut

GASOLINE ROTARY
16" to 24" cut

Scissors cut

Scissors cut

Knife cut

THE LINE-UP. Here are three representative kinds of lawn mowers that you may choose from. There are a few other basic kinds of mowers, but those shown here and described below do the best job on lawns

mowers available. These machines are available to anyone. They cost more than ordinary mowers but they do such a good job on Bermuda that some homeowners find them worth it.

All reel mowers throw their cuttings out in one diagonal direction. They go to the right if the blades twist as in the mower in the picture above, and to the left if the spiral goes the other way.

If you use a reel mower without a basket (see pros and cons on page 46), mow in a counter-clockwise direction if your mower throws to the left, clockwise if it throws to the right. That way the mower will deposit part of its clippings on uncut grass. On the next parallel trip, the mower will chop up some of the previous run's clippings. Finely cut clippings sift down into grass better than long pieces.

If you follow the remove-the-clippings school, you may prefer a reel mower just because you can attach a basket to it. With most old-fashioned rotary mowers, you must rake or sweep your clippings after you finish mowing.

Any reel mower is a precision instrument; it deserves careful treatment. Each time you mow, listen to the cutting sound. Is it the same as last time? A clanking can mean a blade out of alignment; have your lawn mower service man adjust it. Squeaking or stiff action usually means it needs oil. Use a light household oil; if it's for lawn mowers, the label will say so. Is the mower cutting evenly? If it leaves rough spots or if tough blades of grass pass through the blades unscathed, the blades are probably dull or out of alignment or both. If the blades revolve too rapidly, they are probably not set close enough to the cutting bar.

THE POWER REEL MOWER

Most power reel mowers are self-propelled; the engine drives the reel and also the wheels. (The self-propelled feature is less usual on rotary mowers.)

Two features suit the power reel mower to hilly lawns: it fits into contours; the power-driven wheels take it up slopes and hold it on course across slope.

A power reel mower generally costs about $20 more than a power rotary mower of the same cutting width and same kind of engine and same manufacturer.

A power reel mower is somewhat safer to operate than a rotary mower but the difference is only relative. No machine with power-driven, fast-moving blades is safe.

The power reel mower is a lawn mower only. It is not so efficient as the gasoline-powered rotary when it comes to high grass, tall weeds, rough ground, chopping debris, and chopping up leaves on the lawn.

REEL. Medium-price model has five blades. As each blade moves over cutting bar, it snips band of grass. Roller levels cutting bar, adjusts it for mowing height

STRIPED LOOK. The reel mower, either power or hand-operated, leaves a striped pattern which remains visible for about three days after the grass is mowed

THE POWER ROTARY MOWER

Unlike the scissors action reel, the rotary cuts like a scythe or knife. The rotary blade shown in the photograph is one of several types. Some have sickle bar sections or freely pivoting blades mounted at the end of the big blade or at the edge of one or two horizontal discs. The sickle bar sections and freely pivoting blades are easy to sharpen or replace.

All rotaries cut only with the outer inch or so of the rotating piece, whether it is the sharpened edge of the big propellor-like blade or a specially mounted knife.

Until recently all rotaries left clippings on the grass. To collect such clippings, you must rake or sweep. The clippings, however, are chopped finer than is usual with a reel mower, and so are perhaps less likely to trouble your lawn if left in place. Now rotary mowers are being manufactured that accommodate a catching bag—like on a vacuum cleaner.

Two outstanding advantages of the rotary mower are its ability to cut high weeds, stalks, and grass, and its ability to trim close to trees, walls, and other obstructions. Also, it can chop leaves on the lawn to the point where you can't see them.

The rotary's height of cut differs from the reel. You can adjust it higher; you can't set it as low. Some of the more expensive models make height adjustment very easy. You just twist a big knob on top of the machine to raise and lower the blades. Usually, you change cutting height by raising or lowering the wheels.

Unlike the reel mowers, the rotary mower will cut while traveling in either direction. This makes it easier to handle, particularly on small or intricate lawn areas. Some rotaries have a flip-over handle; you can make a return trip in the opposite direction without turning the machine around.

A well-made, large, gasoline-powered rotary is usually tougher than the typical reel type or electric-powered rotary. It can stand rough treatment that would damage a reel. Rotary blades can kick into rocks and sticks, knock them out, and not kill the engine. (Some rotaries do throw rocks out some distance and at considerable speed. This may be a hazard.) Nicks and cuts in the blades are not of great consequence because you can file them sharp again. (You should never even think of filing a reel mower's blades.) If, after rough use, the rotary blade looks too hopeless to file, replace it.

A sharp rotary blade requires less power to operate and makes a cleaner cut. Dull rotary blades "mash" the grass tips, leaving a brownish cast on the cut surface. This is especially true with tough grasses.

The horizontal blade arrangement makes most rotary mowers less capable than a reel mower on a contoured lawn. And at low heights a rotary-cut lawn seldom looks quite as neat as a reel-cut lawn (see photographs). With

SCALLOPED LOOK. Rotary mowers may make a track of semi-circular scallops which show for several days. Rotary-cut lawn seldom looks as neat as reel-cut lawn

ROTARY. One of many blade arrangements. All rotaries cut with outer 1½ inches of the rotating piece. Some have detachable knife pieces mounted at ends of blade

a high cut, the opposite is often true.

The typical rotary takes a little more storage space than the typical reel.

ELECTRIC OR GASOLINE POWER?

Among rotary mowers you can choose between electric and gasoline power. Most powered mowers sold today are gasoline driven.

The advantages and shortcomings of the electric machine are briefly stated. An electric rig is limited, sometimes drastically, by its total length of cord and the power and speed of its motor. Usually, you must cut the lawn in a back and forth pattern, gradually working away from your outdoor electric outlet to keep from snarling (or mowing) your cord. If your lawn is very large or far removed from an electric outlet, or if there are many trees on the lawn or between the lawn and the outlet, an electric mower may be unworkable or too much trouble.

The motors on most electric mowers turn noticeably slower than those on gasoline mowers. That means you can't use them for heavy-duty, tall weed cutting as well as you can a gasoline-powered rotary.

On the other hand, the motor is quiet, easy to start, and completely without fumes. On some small lawns, it does the job easily and quickly. Many women like its quietness, preferring this type to the noisy gasoline-powered varieties.

ABOUT THE LAWN MOWER DEALER

When you shop for a powered mower, a knowing dealer can help you select the proper horsepower and cutting width for your needs. The heavier the grass or weeds that you must cut and the faster you push the machine (if it's a rotary), the more power you need.

In the long run, you will probably be happiest with your lawn mower if you buy it from a dealer who will demonstrate it before you take it home and will check you out on its maintenance. We have heard of cases where people bought 4-cycle, gasoline-powered mowers without receiving any instructions or checkout from the dealer whatsoever. The new owners shortly burned out the engines because nobody told them that the crankcases were without oil.

Remember to ask the dealer to show you how to fix the engine in fall if you are going to put the machine in storage for the winter.

YOU CAN'T MOW WET GRASS

Grass with dew or rain or sprinkler water on it will mash under the mower wheels, stick to the blades, and slither under the mower. Unless the ground below is soaked (in which case you should wait until it dries), you can make a wet lawn ready for mowing by brushing it with a sweeper, a piece of burlap, or a tree branch. All that seems necessary is to knock the drops of water off the grass blades. A front-throwing reel mower can cut wet grass with no special preparation.

CUT LOW, CUT HIGH?

Debates about how high to cut "grass" are really rather silly because all "grass" does not respond the same to various cutting heights. There are grass types that must be cut low and grass types that are best cut medium or high. The turf grass variety charts on pages 11 to 14 tell the best cutting heights for each of the main grass types.

It stands to reason that a creeping grass such as bent or Bermuda should be mowed low to keep the runners from piling up and gradually developing into a brown thatch layer. Not so obvious, but as understandable when explained by a plant physiologist, is the need of Kentucky bluegrass plants to keep their central crowns intact—crowns that can be chopped off by blades set lower than 1 inch.

This is all fine but what about grass mixtures of, say, bent grass (3/4-inch mowing height) and Kentucky bluegrass (1 1/2-inch mowing height)? You cannot, over the years, do right by the needs of both grass types. In such a combination, high mowing would favor the Kentucky blue and possibly hold the bent in check. Low mowing would weaken and gradually eliminate the Kentucky blue, eventually leaving you with a bent grass lawn. Since Kentucky blue is relatively easy to live with and bents demand care, practical and/or lazy homeowners might intentionally mow such a mix at 1 1/2 to 2 inches and thereby encourage the Kentucky blue and discourage the bent (which, for warmer climates, probably shouldn't have been in the mix in the first place). It would be selective graminicide; nothing illegal about it.

The need for low mowing of Bermuda grass and zoysias cannot be overemphasized. In the Bermuda areas, no turf looks as neat as a Bermuda mowed low—almost shaved you might say—at 1/2 inch. And the opposite extreme, high-mowed Bermuda looks and feels about as sloppy as turf can get—mounding, runners showing, an inch or two of yellow-brown thatch between the soil and the green grass surface.

HOW FREQUENTLY TO MOW?

Some theories say that you should mow frequently enough so that at no time will the mower remove more than 1/3 of the total leaf surface. Cutting off a greater portion of grass blade is supposed to cause a physiological shock to the plant because production of food is curtailed. The theory has not always held up experimentally.

In practice, it is sometimes hard to avoid cutting off more than 1/3 of the leaf blade—especially when a lawn has been fed within the past two or three weeks and the person who mows the lawn can only do it once a week. Don't worry about cutting too deep when that happens. On the other hand, don't make a habit of cutting a tall hay crop on the lawn every three weeks or so. That kind of practice would definitely weaken the growth.

SHOULD YOU LEAVE THE CLIPPINGS?

If you are going to leave the clippings on the lawn, mow promptly when the lawn is ready. The clippings then are short and will drop between the grass blades without being very conspicuous.

In dry-summer areas clippings sifted into the grass don't always decay as fast as they might. Too often they mat beneath the grass and just compound the problem of thatch, the tightly woven layer of stolons and grass bases that forms between the soil and the green grass blades. Tight thatch sometimes makes water run off and prevents fertilizer from going into the soil solution. It also raises the height of the mower, making it increasingly difficult to mow as the season progresses.

If you take the clippings off in a basket, with a rake, or in a sweeper, you have a disposal problem, particularly if you gather a good quantity of clippings.

WHERE TO DUMP GRASS CLIPPINGS

The best thing you can do with the clippings is compost them or spread them in a thin layer over the surface of garden beds to act as a moisture-holding, weed-checking mulch. The most impractical thing you can do with them is dump them in the garbage can—especially if your garbage can is barely adequate for the household garbage, if pickups are infrequent, or if you pay for garbage collection on a weight or per-can basis. The worst thing you can do is pile the clippings in a big heap in the corner of your garden or put them in a box or barrel to take out to the dump one of these days.

WHY NOT PUT THE GRASS IN A PILE?

A three-foot pile of grass clippings appears to be harmless. The grass on the surface turns brown and the pile, representing several weeks' mowings, looks like a suburban version of a haystack. But it isn't. Except during the frost season, it breeds flies!

If you don't believe that a pile of grass can be a fly breeding place in spring, summer, and fall, stick a spade under the stack, turn it over, and behold what's going on inside. We've done this; it is not a pretty sight at all.

SWEEPER GATHERS LEAVES before mowing and makes stems and stolons stand up to be chopped. It does a fast job of picking up clippings after mowing

USE CLIPPINGS for composting or mulching. Sack can be removed from the sweeper and carried to compost pile or bed. Thin layer of clippings makes good mulch

As many as 3,000 house fly larvae (maggots) have been found in a single pint sample of decomposing grass —perennial ryegrass, Kentucky blue, bent, clover, and other species.

The house fly is just one of four types of fly collected as larvae from piled lawn clippings. Others: false stable fly, soldier fly, and the lesser house fly. The lesser house fly is the little one that flies around and around in the middle of the living room or beneath the patio overhead and seldom alights. The regular house fly rests on the table, flies a little, and then rests some more.

It doesn't take long for flies to develop in piled grass. Adult flies can emerge from a breeding place in as little as six days after the eggs were laid. And this can happen in grass clippings piled only two inches deep.

At the bottom of a pile of grass clippings a week old, or older, you will also discover that the grass has turned into a slimy, yellowish-brown, odorous mass. It does this because it has a high water content when cut, and the clippings, piled flat together, leave little or no room for air. High water content plus low air content encourage development of anaerobic bacteria. They are the smell-producing bacteria. The opposite faction, the aerobic bacteria, work where air is present and bring about decomposition just as fast, or faster, without producing bad odors. Aerobic bacteria are the ones that work for you breaking

down vegetable material in a properly functioning compost pile.

CAREFUL COMPOSTING IS ALL RIGHT

Naturally, if you pile three or four basket loads of clippings on top of your compost pile and just leave them there, you get just what you get from a grass pile in a corner—flies and bad smells. But if you turn the clippings frequently (every two or three days) and water after each turning, the anaerobic bacteria will never get a real foothold. Decomposition will take place fast, courtesy of aerobic bacteria. In a short time, you will get a clean, nutrient-rich compost from your clippings.

Or you may throw the clippings on the pile in alternate thin layers with leaves, plant tops, or weeds. Or you may mix the rough vegetation with the clippings. Either method insures air spaces and lessens the chance for anaerobic stagnation.

SPREAD CLIPPINGS THIN AS A MULCH

If you have several large beds of shrubs, dahlias, roses, strawberries, or anything that doesn't cover the ground completely, you might spread the grass clippings over the soil beneath them. The grass will check water evaporation from the surface and discourage weed growth to a degree. Each week, spread the clippings on another bed. If, at this rate, you can work your way back to the original bed

PROFESSIONALS USE THIS to mow up to a wall and slice lawn edges. Rotary mowers can cut along walls, around trees and other obstructions as this device does

HAND-OPERATED EDGER. Rotating wheel pulls grass across the cutting edge, quickly trims edges of lawn. Power models do not require a hard edge to run on

in two or three weeks, the original bed will then be ready for another mulching. A thin layer of grass clippings (no deeper than one inch) dries up in a short time and almost disappears.

THE FINISHING TOUCHES

To put a fine finish on a newly mowed lawn, mow a second time in an opposite direction. Or mow diagonally the second time. If there is a big crop of clippings to rake or sweep after the first mowing, collect them before your second mowing. The second time around you will chop off the runners the rake or sweeper pulled up.

A sweeper (see photograph on page 47) works like a king-size carpet sweeper to do a fast easy job of picking up clippings. It also will do an excellent job of sweeping up leaves. If it's an adjustable-height model, you can lower the brushes to sweep the patio and driveway. You can buy a wind cover for the open part of the basket to keep leaves and clippings contained on a windy day.

Since grass spreads horizontally, you need a tool to edge lawn sides. Hand shears or a stout old knife will do the job, but slowly and tediously. For a few dollars you can get a hand-operated edger, with a rotating wheel that pulls grass across an upright cutting edge. This device calls for a hard surface on the outside of the lawn edge to support the rubber drive wheel and give traction to turn the cutting wheel. A double wheel on this kind of edger makes it possible to use on a soft surface.

A power edger will slice the edge of a lawn without any pushing or need for traction. It is especially useful for large lawns and for lawns that adjoin flower beds without any dividing strip. If you take the blade off a power lawn edger and replace it with a wire wheel brush made for a power drill, the wire brush will do a very nice edging job. And, it won't cut into wooden dividers, header boards, sprinkler heads, fences, and walls as the regular metal blade can do. Blade or brush uses its speed rather than sharpness to do the edging. So the wire brush cuts just as neat an edge as the blade.

In addition, the wire brush will do some things that the blade won't do. It cleans up the surface below—wood, concrete, or brick that was beneath the untrimmed grass before edging looks clean and new after brushing. Also, the brush can do its work alongside a sprinkler head, or at a place where a divider board makes a right-angle or a T with another board—the usual edging blade gets a little difficult to handle at such junctures.

Get a wire wheel brush of the same diameter as the overall length of the edger blade. Most edger blades are 6 inches long. The 6-inch diameter is common among wire wheel brushes.

Weeds and Weed Killers

If we always grew only what we thought we sowed originally in a lawn, the whole business of lawn keeping would be a lot easier. The trouble is that soils generally are full of dormant weed seeds—waiting for the right conditions to make them sprout. Furthermore, it is almost impossible for a batch of lawn seeds to be 100 per cent pure. Harvesting at the seed farms brings in some foreign seeds. Blowers, sifters, and machines at the seed company plants take most of them out again; but a few get through, and you sow them with the grass seed. In addition wind, birds, and foot traffic are forever bringing new seeds to a lawn.

So, we will always have weeds. But how about ways to get rid of them? There was a time when lawn weeding meant crawling about on hands and knees pulling, digging, and prying out the foreign plants among the lawn grass. Now, at least three-fourths of that has been eliminated by the selective weed-killing chemicals. One group of selective weed killers can wipe out all the broadleafed weeds. The other group kills some but not all grassy weeds. Naturally, research chemists find it harder to develop a chemical that will kill all the unwanted grasses but leave the lawn grasses alone. Weedicide selectivity is based chiefly on the differences between the physical make-up of plants, and, after all, all grasses are pretty similar. The fact that there now are chemicals that can select and kill crabgrass and dallis grass (weeds) among grasses that man chooses to call "lawn" is indeed impressive.

The weeds and the weed-killers in the two classes (broad-leafed and grassy) are absolutely different and need to be discussed separately. For that reason, you will find broad-leafed weeds pictured and discussed on pages 50 to 54; the grassy ones on 54 to 58. First, however, let us take a brief look at the devices with which either kind of weed killer can be applied.

WEED KILLER APPLICATORS

Compared to the old days when every lawn weed had to be removed personally with a prying tool, the eradicating gadgets available today raise this operation nearly into the sport class. You can choose among an array of applicators that will squirt, spray, sprinkle, douse, or dust offending weeds with the pull of a trigger or twist of a valve.

Here are five choices in apparatus to use for spot application of a weed killer:

1. Applicator wands are designed for spot application of chemicals to individual weeds. You merely fill the chamber of the plastic or steel contrivance with the liquid weed killer, place the business end of the wand over the weed, and press the plunger. This type of applicator has the advantage of limiting the dose to a small area and thus avoiding drift to other plants.

2. Children's squirt pistols or water guns are remarkably useful for applying spot dosage to the crown of weeds. Lock up the pistol, of course, to keep it away from the small fry. Weed killers can be very dangerous if the pistol falls into young hands. Attach a permanent poison label to the weapon.

3. Trigger-type squirting oil cans, obtainable in automobile supply stores will do a fine job of spot application. Clean the can out with household ammonia and water after using 2,4-D and its relatives, so the can will be clean and ready for use next time a weed shows its head. Keep one can exclusively for herbicides; and to prevent your inadvertently oiling the car with weed killer, paint the can a distinctive color to separate it from its fellows.

4. Mops, swabs, or paint brushes work quite easily for spot control. Just dip the swab or brush into a can or bucket of label-directed solution and daub it onto the weeds you want to kill.

5. You can buy wax bars containing a weedicide mixed into the wax. You rub the bar over the weeds.

And, here are three kinds of devices for applying a selective weed killer evenly over the entire lawn:

1. Hose-end applicators are obtainable in several styles that can be attached to the garden hose to apply water-soluble chemicals. Apply with a low pressure in order not to wash all the weed killer off the leaves. Just a coarse wetting spray is all that's needed. If you are accustomed to applying insecticides and liquid fertilizers with similar

devices, you would be prudent to keep a separate one for herbicides. Otherwise, there is always the chance that a few stray particles of the weed killer will be lodged in the contrivance and may become mixed with the insecticide or fertilizer and damage plants that you are treating.

2. Pressure spray tanks and watering cans are excellent devices for applying weed killers, but once they have been filled with 2,4-D or 2,4,5-TP, they should not be used for any other purpose than weed eradicating. If your weed problem is serious or if you have a great deal of territory to treat, you might feel that the expense of buying a pressure spray tank would be justified. For most gardeners, however, simpler devices listed above serve as well or better than these relatively expensive dispensers. If you do use spray tanks or watering cans, clean them out after use with a solution of household ammonia and water, or a patented spray tank cleaner preparation.

3. Dry fertilizer spreaders, shown on page 62, provide an efficient means of applying dry or granular weed killers—packaged by themselves or in combination with a dry fertilizer.

CAUTIONS ABOUT WEED KILLERS

Knowing how a chemical works is the very best guide on how to use it.

If a perennial weed is "killed" merely by contact (severe leaf burn), it may grow back again from its vigorous root system. But if the same weed is attacked by a chemical that it takes in through its leaves and moves down into its stems and roots, it may be killed forever.

Crabgrass can be taken out of a lawn with a contact chemical, one that moves through the leaves, or one that kills the germinating seeds. No one method is better than others, but each has its best-time use because of the way it works, and you may prefer one to the other. For example, many chemicals that work on the germinating seeds don't discolor grass, and that is important.

PAINSTAKING IS THE WORD

Remember at all times that it is all-important to get the right chemical for the right job, at the right time, with the right amount applied in the right way under the right conditions. Ignore one of these steps and you'll waste time and money, and perhaps lose some plants.

If you use a chemical that kills weeds as they germinate, don't expect it to work unless you cover every inch of soil. If a breeze comes up while you are spreading dust or granulars or spraying a selective weed killer, don't

continue and hope for the best. Wait for the wind to stop and then apply the material.

If using a weed killer that is taken up by the leaves of weeds, don't assume that if a little is good, a lot is better. Over-doses may burn down or kill the leaves and thus prevent proper translocation, or movement, down to the root system. And too large a volume of spray may wash the chemical off the leaves rather than just wetting them.

Spot treatment, using a small paint brush or sponge on a stick to "daub" a weed, permits use of such chemicals with greater safety. For example: 2,4-D to kill dandelion, etc., in dichondra, or dalapon on Dallis grass or rye grass clumps in lawn.

HIRE IT DONE

In a few home gardens, weed infestations and soil diseases are such that the cheapest and most sensible thing to do is to completely fumigate or "pasteurize" the soil with a chemical designed to do the job (this is discussed on page 58), and start all over. In such cases, the safe way is to call in a professional to do the job.

THE BROAD-LEAFED WEEDS

This term "broad-leafed" is used considerably by horticulturists and gardeners and its literal translation is not exactly its meaning. When a gardener talks about broad-leafed evergreens he means any tree or shrub that keeps its leaves through the winter but isn't a conifer with needle leaves. In talking about lawn weeds, the term broad-leafed is used to describe any non-grassy weeds.

"Broad-leafed," then, does not necessarily mean possessing a leaf that is notably broad in its dimensions. Quite the contrary; chickweed and spotted spurge, for instance, have leaves about the size of birds' eyes but both are broad-leafed weeds . . . because they are not grass-like.

The chemical killers of broad-leafed weeds

The hormone type weed killers—2,4-D and 2,4,5-TP—are the best known of the herbicides. They kill broad-leafed plants by speeding growth so that the plants literally grow themselves to death. One or the other of the two closely related chemicals (or a combination of them) can kill any broad-leafed lawn weed, but the different weed species vary in their susceptibility. Many broad-leafed weeds collapse with one shot, some take two treatments, some take three or more. Some weeds must be given stronger mixtures than others.

This type of chemical is absorbed by the leaves and carried through the vascular system to the roots. Both

COMMON DANDELION   **COMMON PLANTAIN**   **CURLY DOCK**

tops and roots are killed. Weeds treated with the chemicals show curled and twisted stems in the first stages.
Finally, the roots are expanded and ruptured and the
entire plant dies. The chemicals are most effective at a
temperature of 70° and are ineffective below 50°.

You will notice on the shelves at nurseries and garden
stores that some 2,4-D-type weed killer labels say "kills
common lawn weeds," or "destroys weed." Yet other
labels make quite a display of the fact that the contents
will "kill oxalis" or "kill chickweed." The reason is that
2,4-D, the original broad-leafed weed killer, didn't always kill some of the tougher broad-leafed weeds such as
oxalis and chickweed. The later entry, 2,4,5-TP, did a
better job on these difficult ones. So, they announce it
loudly on the label.

The fact that 2,4,5-TP will kill mouse-ear chickweed
or oxalis where plain 2,4-D won't does not mean that
2,4,5-TP is a stronger weed killer. It's just that those
two weeds (and a few others) are more susceptible to the
2,4,5-TP chemical than to 2,4-D. The 2,4-D is just as
effective a weed killer as 2,4,5-TP when used on the weeds
that are susceptible to it.

A new selective weed killer for killing clover, chickweed, yellow oxalis, plantain, and knotweed in bent
and bluegrass lawns is MCPP. It is claimed to be as
active as 2,4,5-TP but less toxic to some of the grasses.

A caution: Most garden plants are just as susceptible
to these weed killers as are dandelion and plantain.
Therefore, the chemicals should be handled with great
care. Apply the liquid forms at low pressure to avoid
drift to other plants, and in a sprayer that is used for no
other purpose, because the residue can contaminate garden sprays mixed in the same tank.

Broad-leafed weeds in dichondra lawns

Naturally, you cannot broadcast any of the broad-leafed
weed killers intended for grass lawns on a dichondra
lawn because this turfing plant is, itself, a broad-leafed
plant. To treat oxalis or any of the other broad-leafed
weeds in dichondra, apply one of the broad-spectrum
selective weed killers for dichondra lawns, described on
page 79.

Meet the worst ones

Here are descriptions of some of the worst broad-leafed
weeds—how they grow, which member of the 2,4-D
family to use, physical methods of getting rid of them.
Where repeat applications are suggested, wait at least
three weeks between applications. A one or two week
interval can damage the grass. Remember that 2,4,-D and
its family kill slowly so don't despair too soon. Wait and
treat regrowth when it shows up.

Sheep sorrel, dock *(Rumex* species). These weeds
make serious trouble in lawns and garden beds. Their
tenacious root systems remain in the earth and grow even
after you pull the plant tops off. The weed pictured above
is curly dock. Its husky, brownish taproot may go down
2 feet or more before stems show above ground. Sheep
sorrel, a close relative, has arrow-shaped leaves and
spreading roots. *Control:* Curly dock is susceptible to
2,4-D or 2,4,5-TP although there may be regrowth requiring retreatment. The sheep sorrel probably is more susceptible to mixtures containing 2,4,5-TP. A very troublesome but sure method of control is to dig out the roots
and the rootstocks that grow outward.

Common or broadleaf plantain *(Plantago major)* and
buckhorn plantain *(P. lanceolata).* Common plantain
is pictured above. Buckhorn has longer, narrower, more

ENGLISH DAISY   MOUSE-EAR CHICKWEED   YELLOW OXALIS

pointed leaves. The plantains aren't as difficult to get rid of even though they are widespread and persistent. *Control*: 2,4-D or MCPP is fairly sure to control them. The roots are shallow and fibrous and come up easily if you pry up or dig them out with a strong knife.

Common dandelion *(Taraxacum officinale)*. This old enemy needs no introduction. Reason it's such a pest is because its downy seeds blow in all directions and germinate easily. Plants grow so flat that the mower goes right over them. *Control*: It is very susceptible to 2,4-D or 2,4,5-TP treatment. If you have only a few dandelions, try spot treating them with a swab or applicator to save trouble of spraying. They don't pull easily because leaves grow so flat, but if you can get a prying tool underneath the leaf cluster, they come up with little resistance.

Perennial mouse-ear chickweed *(Cerastium vulgatum)*. This is the only weed you can find in some well kept lawns. It grows in among the grass blades and isn't always obnoxious. However, it has a different color and texture. *Control*: It is almost impossible to pull, but repeated use of 2,4,5-TP will kill it. Neburon is effective on established lawns (turf less than a year old may be killed by it). MCPP works, too.

English daisy *(Bellis perennis)*. English daisies in a lawn are good or bad, depending on your feeling toward them. Some people plant and encourage them there for a meadow effect and for their pink and white flowers in spring. *Control*: Leaves lie under mower, but you can pull plants with a prying tool. 2,4-D and 2,4,5-TP give excellent control.

Wild or cut-leafed geranium *(Geranium dissectum)*. This is really a pretty little weed when it flowers, but like mouse-ear chickweed, it mars a perfect texture. *Control*: Susceptible to 2,4-D and it pulls rather easily if ground is moist.

Yellow oxalis *(Oxalis corniculata)*. It seems to have roots all along its stems, so that pulling is next to impossible. *Control*: Several successive applications of MCPP or 2,4,5-TP will kill it. It has been discouraged by heavy applications of ammonium sulfate, and by digging out plants early and burning them. Force lawn grasses to smother it. If a dichondra or grass lawn is interwoven with oxalis, try the neburon treatment outlined on page 79.

Common chickweed *(Stellaria media)*. Chickweed is an annual that usually starts with the first fall rains. It dries up in exposed places when weather warms but continues in moist places. Pulling is easy but slow and tedious. *Control*: Successive applications of 2,4,5-TP will kill it. MCPP is effective, as is neburon on established lawns. Try to kill the chickweed when it is young and tiny.

Bur clover *(Medicago hispida)*. Gather all the runners to the plant's central crown and pull up firmly and slowly from moist ground (immensely satisfying experience). *Control*: It is susceptible to 2,4,5-TP. When the weed is growing vigorously, 2,4-D will work.

Pennywort *(Hydrocotyle umbellata)*. A native perennial, especially bothersome in Southern California. It spreads from slender rootstocks. Its circular leaves are about 1/2 inch in diameter and have scalloped margins. Leaf stalk is attached at center of leaf. *Control*: Apply 2,4-D or MCPP.

BUR CLOVER

COMMON CHICKWEED

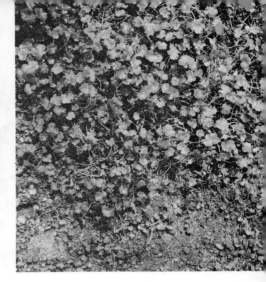

PENNYWORT

False dandelion *(Agoseris apargioides,* formerly *A. hirsutz).* This is a perennial herb that would grow a foot high if it escaped the mower blades. It has the same general habit of growth, leaf shape, and flower head as the true dandelion. Both dandelions have yellow flowers, but in false dandelions they are tinged with red or brown underneath. *Control:* Apply 2,4-D.

Hairy cat's ear *(Hypochoeris radicata).* This perennial weed grows from a thick fleshy taproot. It forms a flat surface cluster of dark green, toothed or cut leaves that are covered with stiff yellowish hairs. Left unmowed, it will send up several wiry, 1 to 2-foot stalks that bear 1 to several long-stemmed yellow flower heads. *Control:* Repeated applications of 2,4-D.

Yarrow *(Achillea millefolium).* A hairy perennial herb that grows from rootstocks. Has soft, gray-green, fern-like foliage with a bitter aromatic scent. Although grown in gardens for its everlasting flowers, it is out of place in a lawn. *Control:* Dig out at first sign as it spreads slowly by underground rhizomes. Repeated sprayings of 2,4,5-TP will give control.

Spurges *(Euphorbia* species). Several spurges cause trouble in lawns. Thyme-leaf spurge (*E. serpyllifolia*) and spotted spurge (*E. supina*) are the worst offenders. Both have soft, little, round leaves that may be all green or green spotted with red, and both grow in low ground-hugging mats with dozens of tiny flowers among the leaves and at the ends of the stems. Each plant deposits

CUT-LEAFED GERANIUM

COMMON KNOTWEED

Smooth crabgrass
(Digitaria ischaemum)

Hairy crabgrass
(Digitaria sanguinalis)

hundreds of hard round seeds on the ground beneath it. Grows in sparse areas in lawns—where bad growing conditions might have weakened the grass—and in walks, driveways, and similar places. A much-branched root system goes 15 feet down, supplying the plant with continual moisture. A good food storage system is an added feature that makes spurge difficult to kill, but if you use 2,4,5-TP often enough, you kill it. The weed is most vulnerable to chemicals in the younger stages of growth, early in the season. It is hard to wet—you may need to add a little liquid detergent or liquid shampoo to the spray to act as a wetting agent.

Common knotweed, wiregrass *(Polygonum aviculare)*. A persistent annual with slender, wiry, blue-green stems which form prostrate, sparsely leafed mats. Sturdy central root and tough wiry branches make it hard to pull up. Not a grass, regardless of name "wiregrass." Leaves are bluish green or bottle-green. Tiny white flowers grow close to the leaves. *Control:* This weed occurs on compacted soils. It is common, for instance, next to driveways and walls. Try aerifying the compacted areas and feeding to encourage the turf grasses. Responds to MCPP or 2,4,5-TP, especially when the weeds are young. Old, dry, woody plants are very hard to kill.

Hop clover *(Trifolium dubium)*. A forage plant that has invaded lawns with annoying success. It has tiny yellow flowers in heads. *Control:* Pull out of moist ground, or treat with 2,4,5-TP or a mixture of 2,4-D and 2,4,5-TP. Straight 2,4-D is relatively ineffective.

CRABGRASS AND OTHER GRASSY WEEDS

The reference point—the rallying place—for all discussions of grassy weeds has to be the unwelcome summertime monster called crabgrass *(Digitaria ischaemum* and *D. sanguinalis)*. It has to be the reference point because it is the most troublesome lawn weed in most of

North America. It is so troublesome and notorious that every day all summer long, ten thousand lawn-keeping Americans stand on their lawns and point to some other grassy weed and call it crabgrass. That mistaken identity is the second reason why crabgrass must be the rallying place.

It's not that anybody cares if you misname a weed! It's just that you shouldn't buy crabgrass-killing chemicals to apply to some weed that won't even be fazed by such chemicals. The chances are about 100 to 1 that such misapplied chemicals won't do any good; they'll waste your time and money; and you might condemn some perfectly good products as a result. On the other hand, if your lawn really is infested with crabgrass, we want to help you learn how to recognize it and how and when to get rid of it.

Any grass that destroys the even texture and color of a lawn is a weed grass. We could probably let it go at that if crabgrass hadn't received so much publicity in recent years. You see crabgrass chemicals advertised everywhere. You hear crabgrass jokes on television. Neighbor-to-neighbor misnaming of other grassy weeds as "crabgrass" spreads like a contagion. (The same is true in certain parts of the southwest with the word "devil grass"—only there the situation is even worse because that term seems to belong to *both* crabgrass and Bermuda grass, and who knows what else?)

In most hot-summer areas, the real crabgrass is truly a wicked summer weed. This is true in the midwest and east, in the hot-summer sections of the southwest and California, and in most communities between the Sierra-Cascades and the Rockies. But it *most definitely is not* a weed of any importance in Florida, in areas along the Gulf of Mexico, west of the Cascades in Oregon and Washington (although it is beginning to show up there), in Alaska, in the cooler parts of California, and in Hawaii.

Some areas are transitional—half way between the

hot-summer (crabgrass) areas and the cool-summer (no crabgrass) areas. In these places, crabgrass shows up in certain isolated lawns, not at all in many others.

How crabgrass grows

Unlike turf grasses and dichondra, crabgrass is an annual. Its reproductive capacity is enormous: a single plant may produce 50,000 seeds. This means that any control, to be effective, must be almost perfect. A few surviving plants will mature enough seed to make a major infestation the following year. And, at that, most of the seeds will remain dormant to sprout some other year.

Some experts have suggested that water mains spread the seeds (crabgrass thrives in an overwatered turf). At any rate the weed is so widespread and produces seed in such huge quantities that you're bound to get it everywhere, by one means or another, once it has a foothold. The hotter your summer, the longer your growing season, the harder it hits.

Crabgrass leaps to life when soil temperatures increase. It begins to germinate at the time spring comes to your area. The progression of crabgrass germination up the Pacific Coast is generally similar to the pattern in the rest of the country: late December and January in Southern California; February to late March in Northern California; April and early May in the interior parts of the Pacific Northwest; July in Seattle.

In almost no time after the fat-leafed seedling spears begin to pepper the lawn, the plants become 3-branched youngsters; and if weather holds warm, they can spread out into ugly, flat clumps in a week. In hot climates, cool-season grasses begin to slow down or go almost dormant at just the time crabgrass hits its stride, so the crabgrass can take over.

At this point, you usually decide to do something about it. At first, you may have a fling at hand weeding. If infestation is heavy, you'll soon realize this is hopeless. The soil is full of last year's seed. Each flat clump you remove only leaves a patch of bare ground or weakened turf for a dozen new seedlings to fill.

From here on, clumps get bigger and bigger. If you keep crabgrass cut short, it doesn't look too bad, and you'll at least have a green lawn up until about November. But at that point it turns reddish brown and dies, leaving you with a full-dress renovation job. Worse yet, the soil is full of seed for next year's crops.

Incidentally, in spring and early summer it is possible to confuse crabgrass with other weeds, but from midsummer until frost there can be no doubt. Only the two forms of crabgrass look like the illustrations on the opposite page, and only those two weeds show a reddish cast in the older parts of the leaves in midsummer, turn reddish brown all over with the first frost (this is a characteristic in bright, sunny climates only), die in winter.

Chemical attack: it differs by seasons

Here, we look at three particular phases of crabgrass growth in terms of seasons to apply the different kinds of controls:

In late winter or early spring crabgrass seeds (much enlarged here) from last year that would otherwise sprout this year can be killed with any pre-emergence crabgrass control product containing any one of these ingredients: azac; balan (or benefin); betasan (or bensulide); and dacthal. These pre-emergence materials *must* be applied *before* the crabgrass seeds germinate.

In spring when crabgrass seedlings have 2 to 4 leaves, kill them by applying crabgrass control products containing any of the following: amine methyl arsonate, disodium methyl arsonate, calcium methyl arsonate. Two or more applications may be needed. These controls may discolor lawn briefly.

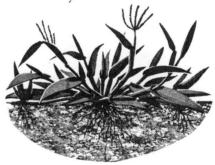

From midsummer into fall, when crabgrass is in its full glory, these chemicals can do the job: disodium methyl arsonate or amine methyl arsonate. Help to increase effectiveness by watering lawn before application and by following up with a second treatment 7 days later.

Good management to discourage crabgrass

Here are some management habits you should develop to discourage reestablishment of crabgrass once you have banished it chemically or to make it difficult for crabgrass to come to your premises:

First of all, water enough each time to wet the full root zone, and then let the surface become dry or nearly dry before the next irrigation. The California Agricultural Extension Service spells it out as "an inch of water at intervals of 3 to 4 days in hot areas and sandy soils, and 2 inches every week or two on loams and heavier soils and in cooler sections." That's a good recommendation for any dry-summer area. Places that get summer rains will have many of these inches supplied for them (too frequently sometimes). Among experts, it is almost unanimous that crabgrass is encouraged by a continually wet soil surface, but is discouraged when surface can dry or nearly dry between waterings.

Feed frequently enough to keep the lawn grass growing vigorously. Give your lawn a feeding once a month starting whenever the cold leaves the ground in your area. It's obvious that an annual weed would find it tough to get established in a lawn in which permanent grass has a thickly-set head start.

In future years, resolve not to let the lawn fall to devitalizing diseases or insects. It's often the case in a lawn that one factor slows growth to a standstill, then the weakened grass quickly takes on all kinds of troubles. Crabgrass (in crabgrass climates) is one of the weakened-turf troubles that you can count on.

The other grassy weeds

It can be just as annoying to the eye to have a lawn full of one of the other grassy or grass-like weeds as having the real crabgrass. However, with the exception of Bermuda in the southern latitudes, and quack grass in many parts of the north, the pretenders are much easier to get rid of.

For one thing, most pretenders can be pulled up more easily. Pull them out or cut them out with a sharp steel knife.

The lawn management suggestions listed above under crabgrass controls also apply to keeping the pretenders out of your lawn.

In chemical controls, all of the pretenders can be killed with spot applications of dalapon or amitrol (Amino Triazole). Apply the chemical directly to the weed grasses, and keep it off the lawn grass as much as possible, because *it will also kill the lawn grasses.* These two chemicals would also work on crabgrass, but crabgrass can take over a lawn to an extent that makes spot applications impractical.

Bermuda grass (*Cynodon dactylon*). In really hot areas, accept it as a lawn because it adapts itself to heat better than the cool-season lawn grasses (Kentucky blue, fescues, bents) and is easier to maintain. Where Bermuda is a weed in a cool-season grass lawn, try grubbing out isolated sprigs. If the infestation gets ahead of you, spot treat with dalapon, like this:

You can increase the effectiveness of dalapon on Bermuda grass by adding a wetting agent to it. If your nurseryman or garden supply dealer can sell you an agricultural wetting agent (there are such things), that's fine. Otherwise, use a detergent such as liquid Vel, dry Tide or All. Make up the label-recommended solution of dalapon. Then, to it add a drop at a time of wetting agent or of detergent mixed with water. Between each drop, dip in a blade of Bermuda grass. When droplets no longer form and the blade comes up covered with an unbroken sheet of the solution, you've added enough wetting agent. Now, spot-apply the mixture to the Bermuda.

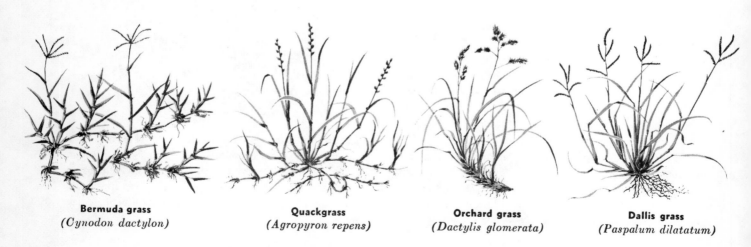

Bermuda grass
(*Cynodon dactylon*)

Quackgrass
(*Agropyron repens*)

Orchard grass
(*Dactylis glomerata*)

Dallis grass
(*Paspalum dilatatum*)

The most effective season for killing Bermuda is in spring when the shoots are just starting to grow. Six weeks after the first application (the original Bermuda will have long since turned brown) start looking for new green Bermuda stems and leaves. If you see any, spot-treat with dalapon and wetting agent again. Repeat a third time in six weeks if necessary. Continue to check and re-treat as long as you can find Bermuda stems and leaves.

Quackgrass (*Agropyron repens*). This weedy grass flourishes in cool, moist, or dry climates, and grows in almost any soil. A perennial, it has slender, straw-colored, scaly rhizomes. These grow about 4 inches below the surface and will extend to 3 to 5 feet. The rhizomes, branching at almost every joint, form a dense root mass, for which the plant is notorious and despised. Any small piece left in the soil will produce a new plant. Do not let this grass go to seed as the seeds are long lived and may lie dormant from 2 to 4 years, then suddenly start new plants. Leaves are dark green in moist climates; in dry areas they are covered with a whitish bloom. The portion of the leaf that sheathes the stem is often hairy. *Control:* Use amitrole (Amino Triazole) according to label directions, or hand-pick or screen out the long white roots from a batch of soil, or treat the area with Vapam (this treatment is discussed on page 58).

Dallis grass (*Paspalum dilatatum*). Since this is often used as a pasture grass, it is a particular problem in some areas recently subdivided from pasture land. Dallis grass is a clumpy, leafy rosette of broad-bladed, bunch grass that is flat, spreading, and has a tendency to die out in the center. Seeds are often introduced in uncured manure. *Control:* Dig out and replace the divot with clean soil, and reseed if necessary. Or you can apply dalapon or diesel oil in crown for fair results.

Annual bluegrass (*Poa annua*). This is a weedy cool-season grass that is encouraged by shade, heavy watering, or weakened turf (look for low-growing ragged seed-clusters and boat-shaped leaf tips). It dies in midsummer, but only after it has broadcast its seed. In Bermuda grass country, annual bluegrass is often sown and cherished because it, like several other grasses, will give green color to an otherwise winter-brown Bermuda lawn. *Control:* Remove the conditions it likes or use dalapon or sodium TCA in careful spot applications. The lead arsenate and calcium arsenate pre-emergence crabgrass controls (page 55) will also control this weed. Pull it. Low mowing can check some—but not all—of the seeding.

Nutgrass (*Cyperus esculentus* and *C. rotundus*). Members of the sedge family with grass-like leaves. Blades are rather broad, bright polished green, trough-like, stiff at first, becoming ribbon-like. They are easily distinguished from the lawn grasses by their 3 tiers of leaves instead of 2, triangular cross-section, solid stems, and no sheaths. They grow from rootstocks which bear tubers or nutlets. If any of these food-storing nutlets are left in the soil after the plant is uprooted, you will get new plants. If allowed to flower, you can readily recognize the umbrella-like clusters topping thick triangular stems. Nutgrasses prefer damp soil, and their appearance in your lawn is often an indication of inadequate drainage. *Control:* This is one of the most difficult weeds to eradicate. See suggestions on use of soil fumigants at the end of this chapter.

Velvet grass (*Holcus lanatus*). This grayish-green fuzzy-bladed grass appears in clumps that gradually enlarge. In early morning, dew held on leaf fuzz makes plants stand out. It will take drought, poor drainage, low fertility, compact soil. *Control:* Spot-treat with dalapon.

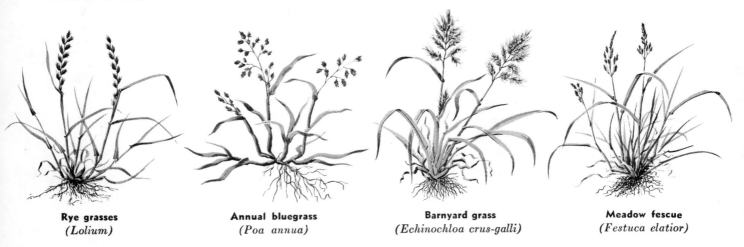

Rye grasses
(Lolium)

Annual bluegrass
(Poa annua)

Barnyard grass
(Echinochloa crus-galli)

Meadow fescue
(Festuca elatior)

Or try changing the poor soil conditions. Or dig it out (same method as for orchard grass).

Orchard grass *(Dactylis glomerata)*. Bunches of coarse, flat blades—sometimes grow horizontally under the mower's cutting level. *Control:* Dig out with a sharp knife, replace divot with clean soil or peat moss and sand, reseed if necessary. Or, spot-treat with dalapon.

Barnyard grass or water grass *(Echinochloa crusgalli)*. The leaf blades are smooth, floppy, and up to ¾ inch wide—one of the coarsest if not *the* coarsest of grassy weeds in lawns. Grows best in very moist soil in the west (it is a pest in rice fields), almost anywhere in the east. *Control:* Same as orchard grass.

Rye grass *(Lolium* species). This is commonly sold as a lawn grass and, by itself or with white Dutch clover, it makes a presentable, shiny-textured lawn. But among fine-textured lawn grasses it looks clumpy, shiny, and coarse. *Control:* Pull it, pare it out, or spot-treat with dalapon or sodium TCA.

Meadow fescue *(Festuca elatior)*. Same situation as rye grass except that meadow fescue makes a coarser lawn—really better for athletic fields than home lawns—and a coarser weed among finer grasses. In a fine-grass lawn, this one looks like a bull in a china shop. The wide coarse blades radiate out from a central point and stay very tight to the ground. *Control:* Same as rye grass.

SOIL FUMIGANTS

There are several chemicals in use that simply sterilize a piece of soil (kill almost everything in it) but in a short time dissipate and leave the soil clean and ready for planting. No poison lingers.

Among these products two should be applied only by professionals. They are too dangerous to be handled by homeowners. Those two otherwise quite recommendable fumigants are methyl bromide and carbon disulfide.

The three fumigants that are safe to use (follow directions and use common sense) are Vapam, Mylone, and calcium cyanamid.

The soil fumigant called Vapam is a water soluble liquid that becomes a gas underground and kills all or most living things in the soil, even nematodes.

Mylone is quite similar to Vapam but you apply it as a dry granular material rather than as a liquid.

The third product, calcium cyanimid is a gray granular substance that you buy in sacks. It kills weed seeds, stolons, and rhizomes (but is not very effective in killing

Bermuda grass); and while killing them it releases two useful soil chemicals: enough nitrogen to supply a new lawn for up to six months; and calcium, which can improve soil structure and water penetration in some soils.

In the northern latitudes, or at least in the Pacific Northwest, Vapam and Mylone have not proved as effective as fungus eradicants as they have in warmer parts of the country. However, the materials are quite effective for weed and insect control there.

How to use Vapam

This is a clear, liquid fumigant that kills weeds, soft or moist weed seeds, stolons, fungus organisms, nematodes.

If the patch you are treating has been dry for some time, soak it several days to a week before treating, to soften the dormant seeds.

DEPTH OF SOAK = DEPTH OF KILL

The label gives you a choice of several ways to apply the chemical, among which these two are the most practical for home gardeners: mixed with water in a sprinkling can (generally the best method), or mixed with water in a pressure tank (no danger of residue as with 2,4-D).

Make sure you apply it evenly. *Do not* apply Vapam under the branches of any valued trees or shrubs. It "root prunes" throughout the soil it penetrates.

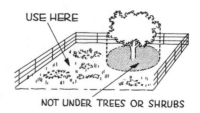

USE HERE

NOT UNDER TREES OR SHRUBS

After you put the solution on the area, water thoroughly to leach the chemical down to the weed root, nematode, and pest level. (Vapam kills weeds only through their roots.) The volume of water for soaking is suggested on the label.

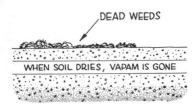

DEAD WEEDS

WHEN SOIL DRIES, VAPAM IS GONE

Soaking also seals surface to contain the gas underground.

Weeds, depending on their constitutions, will die at various rates of rapidity. Gas begins to leave soil when water seal breaks and soil dries a little. Hasten departure by spading on fifth day (no danger to you).

If rain comes during 7 days, you may have to wait longer to replant.

How to use mylone

Mylone is a white powdery material that is carried by water into the soil to kill most weeds and susceptible weed seeds (possible exception: nutgrass). It also controls some nematodes and some soil fungi. It is prepared in various strengths, so watch label directions for the correct amounts to use.

Work soil with a power rotary tiller or a spade several days before treating. When ready, soil should be clod-free and uniformly moist. Apply label-directed amounts, using a fertilizer spreader—in irregular areas apply it by hand but wear gloves. Do not apply the material under the drip line of trees or shrubs. Thoroughly water the powder into the soil (put on approximately 2 to 4 inches of water).

Wait three weeks before planting. Keep soil moist but not saturated during this period.

To make sure it is safe to proceed with planting, plant a few radish seeds in the treated soil. If they sprout and grow normally, proceed with the lawn planting program.

How to use calcium cyanamid

Calcium cyanamid is a compound containing calcium, carbon, and nitrogen. Mixed with soil and watered, it goes through a chemical decomposition that kills germinating weed seeds. Final products of the decomposition are calcium and nitrate nitrogen.

The calcium becomes available to plants and improves soil structure, particularly in soils high in sodium content.

It raises soil pH only temporarily; pH drops back to normal in a few weeks. The nitrate nitrogen from the recommended dosage usually yields nitrogen to supply a lawn as long as 6 months (less if the soil gets great amounts of rainfall or watering).

Directions for using calcium cyanamid to kill weed seeds in the soil when making a new lawn are given on pages 18 and 19.

Treatment for old lawns

If you have an old lawn full of the truly vicious weeds, too thoroughly established to pull or to kill with selective chemicals, do it this way (specific methods for Bermuda, other stoloniferous grasses, and nutgrass are outlined below):

Apply Vapam, Mylone, or cacodylic acid right over the old lawn according to label directions. You don't have to cultivate unless the surface needs regrading. Vapam and Mylone clean up disease spores, which may be present, and any lawn moth larvae, grubs, and weevils, in addition to the vegetation. Wait 7 to 14 days or until soil dries out. Rake or brush new seed into old turf.

2. Or prepare soil first; leave no weeds showing at all. Do everything but seeding or planting. Treat with calcium cyanamid as described on pages 18 and 19 and wait 3 weeks. Expect growth response to extra nitrogen.

Cleanup treatment for new lawns

If the proposed area for a new lawn is full of nothing but weeds, try these alternatives:

1. Prepare soil first (including topsoil and all soil amendments). Do everything but seeding or planting. Treat with Vapam or Mylone, wait 7 to 14 days or until soil dries.

2. Or use diesel oil and hand-grubbing repeatedly.

Cleanup treatment for nutgrass

To correct a bad infestation of nutgrass or sedge, try one of these methods:

1. Pre-soak the area and then have a professional come in and fumigate it with methyl bromide.

2. Thoroughly dry out the soil to tuber level and below. Cultivate deeply to break root connections with moist subsoil. Hand-pick tubers and rootlets. This scheme has worked but it's tedious and difficult.

3. Spray with 2,4-D or weed oil for two or more consecutive years.

Weeding 59

Lawn Fertilizing

When you see grass beginning to turn yellowish or pale green the chances are that an application of almost any lawn fertilizer will get it growing fast and green again. Grass has a continual need for nitrogen, and nature does a poor job of supplying that nutrient in quantities that are adequate to keep grass plants growing thick, green, and dense.

With blessings of several leading lawn experts, we decided to present the creed for lawn upkeep this way in this book:

> If a lawn turns yellow or pale green, if the grass gets thin and weeds come in, it is probably an indication that nitrogen is needed. If you apply a fertilizer containing nitrogen in one form or another and the lawn does not snap out of its doldrums, then suspect some other trouble such as disease, lack of soil air, grubs, or other larvae. But, explore the other possible causes only if the grass does not respond to the nitrogen.

We discuss the other possible causes of paleness, listlessness, manginess in the chapter that begins on page 65. Here we look into the meanings and mysteries of lawn fertilizing.

WHICH FERTILIZER?

Generally speaking, a package of fertilizer that you buy at the store is as good as you make it. Your objective is to keep the grass green by adding the nitrogen the grass plants need at the time they need it. In the three-number formula on a fertilizer label, such as 6-4-2, the first number is the percentage of nitrogen, the second is the percentage of phosphorus, and the third the percentage of potassium. Consider the phosphorus and potassium as bonuses in lawn feeding. The important nitrogen comes in several forms and that is what will be considered here.

The fertilizer manufacturers and packagers formulate mixtures to fit the habits of gardeners as well as the needs of the plant. Therefore, your gardening habits will influence the type of fertilizer you choose. Here are the fertilizers to use for each of several kinds of lawn-feeding programs:

Slow-acting fertilizers

If you are the "once-is-enough type," remember this: In mild climates, grass grows actively too many months in the year to be satisfied with a once-a-year feeding. But if one shot is your limit, your best choice is one of these four kinds of formulations:

1. The slow-acting organics, such as activated sewage sludge, cottonseed meal, hoof-and-horn meal. (Manures and compost are so low in nitrogen that they shouldn't be considered at all. In addition to being weak, they introduce weed seeds, salts, and diseases. These criticisms apply to all manures and composts.)

2. The stabilized inorganics that release their nitrogen slowly.

3. Commercial fertilizers that combine a bulk organic fertilizer and a booster addition of quick-acting (nitrate) inorganic.

4. Regular commercial fertilizer—a balance of nitrogen, phosphorus, and potash.

If you want to go to extremes in reducing lawn maintenance to one application, look to the single-package products that combine a fertilizer, a weed killer, and an insecticide; a fertilizer and a weed killer; or a fertilizer and an insecticide.

Quick-acting fertilizers

If you enjoy giving regular attention to your lawn, the quick-acting fertilizers may suit you best. There's a lot of satisfaction in getting to know the deep green color of a vigorously growing lawn and having the wherewithal to bring it back to the color immediately if it fades to a lighter green.

Important label words

When reading labels, remember this: All organics are not slow acting and all inorganics are not fast acting. The rate of availability grades down from immediate to gradual over a period of months.

Here is the meaning of the words on the label that refer to nitrogen:

Nitrate or nitrogenous—the form of nitrogen that is available to the plant as-is, regardless of temperatures.

Ammoniacal or ammonic—available to plants when converted by bacteria to nitrates. There is evidence of direct utilization, too. Speed of conversion depends upon soil temperatures. It's only a matter of hours in midsummer, but much, much longer when ground is cold.

Organic—describes sludge, cottonseed meal, and any others that must be broken down by bacteria. These are slower than any inorganic form.

Urea—a synthetic organic that water and the enzyme urease change immediately to inorganic ammonia. Conversion to available nitrate follows.

Urea-form or urea formaldehyde—a nitrogen fertilizer that has been specially compounded (stabilized) for slow release.

WHEN TO FEED?

You will find that many beautiful, forever-green lawns are kept that way by the costly process of feeding by the calendar—once a month the year around, whether the grass shows signs of languishing or not.

Timing instructions on fertilizer labels are based on the rate of release of the various forms of nitrogen contained in the fertilizer. A manufacturer of low-nitrogen organic fertilizer will recommend one or two heavy applications and count on the slow release of nitrogen to keep the lawn green. A packager of high-nitrogen, quick-acting fertilizer may advise a full application in spring and fall, or a light application every month or six weeks. The manufacturer of a stabilized nitrogen fertilizer will suggest two long-lasting applications. Several manufacturers make a point of combining fast and slow-acting nitrogen to give the advantage of both.

Remember that more nitrogen must be supplied once each year at the very least and preferably several times each year. Each lawn has its required total. The loss of nitrogen through use or being washed away is fast or slow according to the type of fertilizer used.

It is obvious from the above that the most economical lawn manager is the fellow who sets his own timing application by the appearance of the grass.

The color and the vigor of the grass can show you the nitrogen need. After your eye becomes trained, you can tell well-fed grass from hungry grass by noting the shade of green. Easier than that, you tell the need by the number of times per month or per week the lawn needs cutting. If you find you can let more and more days go by between mowings—first, from 5 days to 8 days, then from 8 days to 14 days, you need to put on more fertilizer. Of course, there is an exception: bluegrass needs a lot of autumn feeding in spite of limited growth at that time.

Depending on the basic fertility of the lawn soil, the grass will show loss of color in from 4 to 8 weeks, or more. Thus, following the when-it-needs-it method, you'll fertilize anywhere from 3 to 12 times a year.

HOW MUCH TO FEED?

The package or sack of fertilizer you buy will carry instructions on how much and when to apply.

If your idea of the correct timing does not coincide with the manufacturer's, you can make your own adjustments in amount to apply at each feeding. University of California recommends 1 pound of actual nitrogen per 1000 square feet per month (when grass is growing —not during the months when ground is frozen or grass is naturally dormant). To figure pounds of "actual nitrogen," take the percentage of total nitrogen, as stated on the label, times the weight of the fertilizer. For example, a 12-pound package of fertilizer (doesn't matter whether it is liquid or dry) containing 17 per cent nitrogen, will yield approximately 2 pounds of actual nitrogen, or enough to feed 2000 square feet for a month or 1000 square feet for two months. The figuring:

$$12 \text{ pounds} \times .17 = 2.04 \text{ pounds.}$$

IRON WHEN NITROGEN DOESN'T WORK

In some parts of the country, notably in California and the Southwest, yellowing of turf that is not corrected by nitrogen may be caused by an iron deficiency. Correct it with one application per year of iron chelate (follow label directions) or iron sulfate (5 pounds per 1,000 square feet — keep it off of concrete and painted surfaces).

FOR GREEN IN WINTER LAWNS

In all mild-winter areas, growth of the hardy grasses never stops completely during winter. In most cases the poor appearance of winter lawns is not due to any kind of physical damage done by low temperatures but to the lack of available plant food. The low temperatures slow up the supply of nitrogen in the ammonia forms because bacterial activity almost ceases. To make a beautiful winter lawn, apply a fertilizer containing a nitrate form of nitrogen in late October or November (as an alternate, use a urea fertilizer). If you are using an organic that must be converted by bacteria, time your late fall feeding to the warmth of the soil. September or early October typically ends the season of fast action by soil bacteria. More often than not, nitrate nitrogen will work even in December and January.

A green dye for coloring winter-browned Bermuda and zoysia is sold by garden supply dealers in Bermuda grass areas. Color-treated grass runs from blue-green to a

HOPPER SPREADER pictured in above three photographs makes the most uniform pattern. Two strips at each end give you room to shut off the spreader, turn, open spreader, and start again. You burn grass if you turn or stop with the hopper open. To avoid gap between runs, overlap previous run's wheel tracks slightly

FOUR COMMON MISTAKES. (1) You can't turn an open hopper inside a previous turn and make a uniform pattern. Overlaps burn grass, and grass stays faded in gaps. **(2)** In the foreground track you see what happens when you stop and start with the hopper open. Walking with an unsteady gait does same thing. Concentrations burn the grass or make it lumpy. **(3)** Strings represent wheel tracks on grass. If you run the inside wheel down the previous run's outside wheel track, you leave an unfed gap between swaths. Even a good rainstorm may not merge the two swaths. **(4)** You shouldn't make 180° turns. One spreader wheel drives the sifter on the inside; the other one turns free. With heavy, pelletized fertilizers, dispersal on such a turn is very erratic

green shade that looks surprisingly natural. You spray the dye over the lawn in a water solution. Most of the products hold color all winter. Rain or sprinkling washes off some dye formulations; others are not affected by water once the dye has dried and set. None of the dyes harms the grass. The manufacturers are very careful to caution the buyer to maintain proper management of the lawn, in spite of the fact that it looks green.

This same dye, by the way, has been used to make a short-of-perfect summer lawn nice and green for a garden party.

FERTILIZER APPLICATORS

Four types of applicators are in general use: The box-on-wheels spreader of dry fertilizers; the tank-on-wheels spreader for liquid fertilizers (on some the pressure is supplied by hand-pumping, on others by wheel drive); the hose attachments for liquid fertilizers, and the hand seeder. You are a fifth type.

The graphic demonstrations in the illustrations show how several of these devices work and what kind of patterns they make.

The chief risk of spreading fertilizer by hand is that

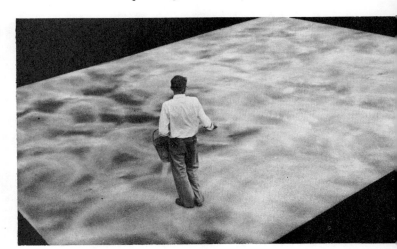

HAND CASTING. If you feed a lawn by hand, do it in a slow and easy manner. Walk with wedding march cadence, synchronize a semi-circular throw with each step

ONE DIRECTIONAL PATTERN (shown at left) is quite spotty, but if you go back over the area crosswise, you will be able to fill out the pattern fairly smoothly

Fertilizing 63

HAND SEEDER. Drop your hat where you start, make a run, and return to hat. Pace off the swath diameter from it to find the starting place for your next parallel run

FULL TILT in no wind, a hand seeder throws pelletized fertilizer over a 20-foot diameter. Left hand operates rate-of-flow lever. At right: closeup of hand seeder

you might hurry the job too much. The places where you throw a whole handful will either burn or come up tufty and greener than the rest of the lawn. You will have to live with this pattern for several weeks, at least.

Be prepared to have the front of yourself thoroughly dusted with fertilizer if you use the hand seeder. It spreads a complete circle.

Hopper spreaders used to have a bad reputation because the store-owned, rented units worked poorly. In recent years, we have noticed that the majority of homeowners who wish to do a good job of maintaining their own lawns buy a spreader and maintain it with the care due to any device that costs from $5 to $30. All-plastic hopper spreaders can be washed out with the hose after use. Metal ones should have the drive wheel turned rapidly to drive out any excess material left in it and then should be dusted out with a cloth. Washing a metal spreader can rust it.

The only limit on hose-end applicators or the tank-on-wheels type is that, for the most part, they are limited to liquids with quick but fleeting action.

WATER AFTER APPLYING FERTILIZER

One final word of advice: If the label on a fertilizer package tells you to water after feeding, please heed that advice—no matter how small the type in which it is said. Only a few dry fertilizers can be applied and then forgotten. Most require a soaking in to get the action started and to prevent burning of the grass blades.

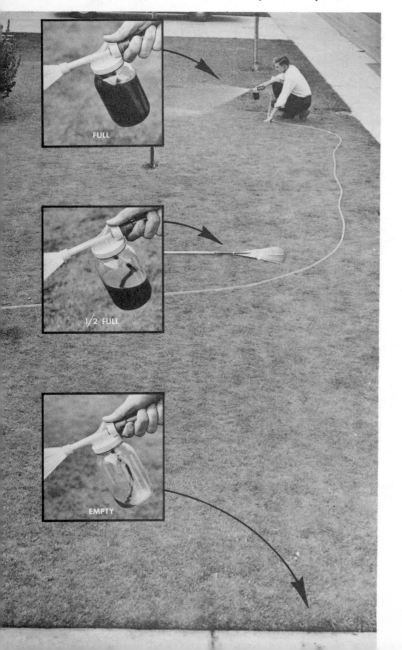

FULL

1/2 FULL

EMPTY

LIQUID FEEDER. Mark halfway point of the area to be covered. Move fast enough to be there when the feeder is half empty and at other end when feeder is empty

Overcoming Lawn Ailments

Sometimes we wonder how many tons of lawn insecticides and fungicides are purchased and used needlessly by well-meaning homeowners whose lawns really need only water or nitrogen fertilizer or both.

Lack of nitrogen makes grass turn yellowish green or pale green, grow slowly, and become thin.

Lack of water makes grass turn limp, then dull and smoky-green, and ultimately die.

Lack of either or both of these two great essentials can lay a lawn open to all kinds of secondary troubles including an array of fungus diseases and insects.

Some lawn discussions state or hint that there is danger from overfeeding or overwatering. We see such a danger as being comparatively remote. In the arid parts of the West, we know it would cost an undue sum of money to overfeed the typical lawn and keep it overfed. In the humid East, bluegrass-fescue-bent lawns can be overfed, especially when the hot weather is approaching. Only certain kinds of clay soils, certain kinds of sunken terrains, or obvious situations such as a lawn on the north side of a wall would allow harmful overwatering. In essence, then, there may be such a possibility but it is unlikely, indeed, alongside the everyday, commonplace fact of underfeeding and underwatering.

Before you attempt to diagnose a lawn trouble, do as a professional turf manager would do—decide if the watering and feeding schedule has been adequate. Should the lawn be fed and watered? These two needs are discussed in previous chapters.

Most of the insects, diseases, and physical troubles of lawns make themselves known by persisting *after* the lawn has been fed with nitrogen and kept adequately watered.

LAWN INSECTS

Two classes of lawn insects do damage to lawns: those that feed on the leaf blades and other *above ground* parts; and those that feed on roots and other *below ground* parts of the grass plant. To know this difference will help make your insecticide applications effective.

Cutworms, sod webworms (lawn moth larvae), skipper larvae, leafhoppers, and chinch bugs (the latter in eastern and southern states) feed above ground. To get them you water the lawn and *then* apply a lawn insecticide, after which you leave the grass alone for a few days until the insecticide does its action.

White grubs, billbug grubs, Japanese beetle grubs (in the eastern states), and soil mealybugs are below-ground pests. To get at them you apply the insecticide and then put on copious amounts of water to drench the material down deep where the insects are.

Anyone who has reason to study lawn pest control much will soon see a great difference between the *modus operandi* for killing lawn insects and that for controlling diseases.

With diseases, as you will see on pages 67 to 70, to prevent is wise and recommendable and to cure is tedious and difficult. Also, selecting the right fungicide for the right disease is a precise matter. With lawn insects, by comparison, you can be really quite casual. Prevention is hardly worthwhile unless, of course, your lawn is attacked repeatedly by the same insect. Then, you'd be only prudent to have some toxic insecticide laying in

FAIRY RING. A dead grass circle expands across the lawn like a ripple in a pool. As ring enlarges, grass in center turns green again. See page 70 for control

DOLLAR SPOT. This fungus disease is indicated by small brown or straw-colored spots in lawn. Spots may enlarge and become one irregular brown area

wait for him the next time. But the need for prevention doesn't come up often.

Selection of an effective lawn insecticide is easy. Sevin and diazinon both work on all of the turf insects, above or below ground. Dibrom, pyrethrum, and rotenone are most effective on the above-surface lawn pests and shouldn't be used for the below-ground insects.

Here are descriptions of the damage done by the leading lawn insects:

Irregular-shaped brown-colored areas: Lawn Moths. If it is a lawn of any kind that is less than two years old, or a bent grass lawn of any age, and especially if tan moths fly over the grass at dusk, suspect lawn moth (sod webworm). The webworms feed on grass crown and bases of blades. The following test will tell you definitely whether it is lawn moth or something else (the most likely other cause is brown patch) discussed later in this chapter.

Mix two teaspoons of pyrethrum or dibrom in one gallon of water, apply it to a square yard of the dying area. If gray worms or caterpillars about ¾ inch long (see illustration) wiggle to the surface within 10 minutes, you have a webworm infestation. In a matted bent grass lawn, it may take a long time for the insects to work their way through. If you can't find pyrethrum or dibrom for the test, use 1 teaspoon of the detergent Vel in a sprinkling can of water to 1 square foot of lawn. University of California at Davis has tried other detergents but for some reason (wetting agent perhaps) Vel works best.

At any rate, if you can bring worms up with one of these tests, apply almost any insecticide. Many have specific directions on the label for sod webworm control. For best results, cut and water the lawn before application. Do not water for at least 48 hours after the treatment so the chemical can dry on the grass blades and grass crowns.

Dead grass in definitely defined patches: White Grubs or Bill Bugs. Pull on the grass. If it comes up like a wet doormat, the cause is probably white grubs. You may even find some grubs underneath the sections you pull up — U-shaped grayish white worms shaped much like fat shrimps. If you aren't squeamish, you can hand-pick the worms from under each patch and know that you have dealt with them in the most direct way. Replace the mat of dead grass. It will grow back in several weeks. Sevin and diazinon are prescribed for best chemical control. If the label mentions white grubs, it will specify a rather heavy dosage. With this chemical treatment, water heavily after application. You have to get the material down to the level where the larvae are eating. You find them most often on lawns under street lights. The light attracts the adults (beetles) at night and they lay their eggs there.

The control for grubs will also control wireworms which you never see but which bore into the underground parts of stems and feed on the roots of grass.

Orange, brown, and yellow butterflies fly over the lawn during the heat of the day: Fiery Skipper. Symptoms, other than the butterflies, are: Isolated round dead spots, 1 to 2 inches in diameter, eventually coalescing and killing large areas of the lawn. Small brownish-yellow worms may be inside the grass within these spots. Sometimes white cottony masses show in the lawn. The white, cottony masses are the cocoons of a parasite which may, by itself, check the skipper's advances. Otherwise, controls are the same as for sod webworms.

Dead spots 1 or 2 inches in diameter, with grass chewed below the mowing level: Cutworms. This pest makes a hole about the thickness of a pencil leading down into the roots. The controls for sod webworm will kill cutworms, too.

Central shoots of grass plants dead: Frit fly. The small, black frit fly has 4 generations of larvae a year. The spring and fall larvae live in young grass stems, eating and eventually killing the central shoots, causing the plant to send out side shoots. Some species of lawn grasses are very susceptible to this pest. Applications of dibrom or diazinon in summer should control it.

Tufting and yellowing of Bermuda grass, plus skin irritation: Bermuda mite. Spray with diazinon several times, or apply 1 pound ammonium sulfate, water in, then apply ½ pound soil sulfur per 100 square feet.

Slugs and snails on the grass at night. Best controls are zectran and the liquid metaldehyde slug and snail sprays. Make a solution and pour it on the lawn through a sprinkling can.

LAWN DISEASES

Sometimes a lawn just begins to die, all over or in patches, and the usual ministrations—careful watering, fertilizing, spraying for lawn moth or grubs—do nothing. The slow death continues. This happens most frequently in summer or early fall although it can happen at any time of the year.

The lawn owner can deduce that if it's not bad watering practice, lack of nutrients, or insects causing his trouble, it must be a fungus. His lawn has been attacked by one or more fungus diseases.

Only rarely does a lawn fungus show the classic symptoms by which you can identify it positively, and then proceed to apply the specific fungicide cure.

Brown patch—much discussed and much pictured—is, for example, a tricky one. The time-worn description says, "smoky ring in an irregular circle surrounding a dead area." But from what we've been able to determine, only a few plant pathologists have ever seen it where it could be recognized by its description.

It's a little easier — but not much — to find a lawn consultant who has really seen dollar spot or helminthosporium in its classic form.

Usually, when you get down on your hands and knees on a sick lawn and compare its symptoms with book descriptions and pictures, you'll find that your lawn fungus could be all or none of several—"brown patch," "dollar spot," "helminthosporium," "fading out," "grease spot," "fusarium patch," or "red thread" — because the symptoms overlap.

In fact, it seems that the diseases themselves overlap. The best diagnosis of the summer malady that gives trouble to fine-bladed grasses in various parts of the country is that it's a complex of helminthosporium and "fading out" (curvularia), with possibly some "grease spot" (pythium) thrown in.

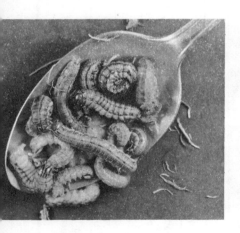  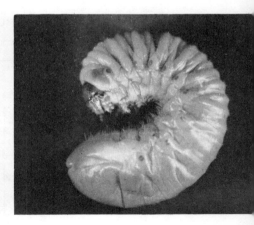

UPPER LEFT: One teaspoon of cutworms can lead to many dead spots in your lawn. Cutworms can consume twice their weight in grass nightly. CENTER: Larvae of lawn moths attack blades. Young larvae skeletonize grass, older larvae attack and cut off blades completely. UPPER RIGHT: These little U-shaped worms are white grubs. You can hand-pick white grubs from affected patches of lawn or use a chemical control

Which Fungicides Work On Which Lawn Diseases

(See opposite page for descriptions of diseases charted)

DESCRIPTION	Product	Helminthosporium Leaf Spot	Fading Out	Grease Spot	Copper Spot	Rust	Brown Patch	Dollar Spot	Pink Patch, Red Thread	Snow Mold	Fusarium Patch	Mushrooms	Moss
These products have mercury compounds as the active ingredients	Calo-Clor						X	X		X	X		
	Calocure						X	X		X	X		
	Semesan				X		X	X		X			
	Phenmad, PMAS, and others (phenyl mercuric acetate)	X	X		X		X	X		X	X		
	Panogen Turf Fungicide	X	X	X	X	X	X	X	X	X			
These are fungicidal compounds found in various products (look for the names on ingredient lists)	cadmium (Cadminate)	X			X			X	X	X	X		
	captan	X		X			X						
	ferbam					X							
	maneb					X							
	PCNB (Terraclor)						X	X					
	Phygon			X		X							
	thiram (Tersan 75 or Thiramad)	X				X	X			X			
	zineb	X		X		X							
These are combinations (more than one active ingredient)	Acti-Dione	X	X	X		X	X	X	X	X			
	Kromad or Formula Z	X	X		X		X	X	X	X			
	Scutl	X	X		X		X	X	X	X	X		
	Tersan OM	X		X	X	X	X	X	X	X			
	Ortho Lawn Fungicides (Coverage varies by region—see label)	X	X	X	X	X	X	X	X	X	X		

(SEE SEPARATE SECTIONS ON PAGES 70 AND 71 FOR DISCUSSIONS OF THESE TWO TROUBLES)

How to use the chart

On the opposite page, we present a list of all turf fungicides likely to be available to home gardeners, charted against all the lawn fungus diseases that are known to occur with much frequency, singly or with other diseases. You can use this chart two ways:

(1) If you can positively identify one of the diseases that is troubling your lawn, use one of the fungicides shown as effective for that disease. The best, most effective practice is to use fungicides as preventives. As curatives, they act slowly.

(2) Or look at the various fungicides to see for yourself which ones are effective on the greatest number of diseases. Then, take a chance that the fungus on your lawn is susceptible to one of these "broad spectrum" fungicides and use that product—as a preventive (preferably) or as a curative (better than doing nothing). Read and follow directions on the label.

Here are descriptions of the various lawn diseases charted. Some of the descriptions are presented with slight tongue in cheek because there are several that rarely if ever show the classic symptoms. The commonest midsummer malady of cool-season grasses from Denver to the coast of California has been diagnosed as a combination of the diseases in the chart's first three columns.

Helminthosporium leaf spot (sometimes called "going out" or "melting out"). First over-all sign, as seen from a distance, is a gradual indefinite yellowing. In infected areas, look for bright yellow leaf blades with brown spots and darkened borders. Eventually the whole leaf turns brown.

Fading out (Curvularia). General yellowing or fading of grass in patches, often surrounding green islands of healthy grass. Tips of grasses turn yellow or tan.

Grease spot (Pythium). Infected blades turn dark and become matted together, giving a greasy appearance in streaks through the lawn. Sometimes a white, cottony mold growth shows on grass blades.

Copper spot (Gleocercospora). Not common. In small areas through lawn, grass blades become covered with orange to copper-colored fungus spores. Rub a white cloth on the spots and it will pick up red.

Rust (Puccinia). Small reddish pustules form on older leaf blades and stems. Blades shrivel and die. Rub a white cloth over a suspected infection; if it picks up orange, it's rust. Feeding to force growth of young leaves seems as effective as any chemical. Maintain regular feeding.

Brown patch (Rhizoctonia). Light attacks result in blackened leaf blades. In heavy attacks, blackened blades form an expanding large irregular smoke ring and the areas look almost as if they were drying out from lack of water. Blades inside the ring become light brown.

Dollar spot (Sclerotinia). Many small (approximately 2-inch) bleached or gray-colored spots. When fungus first starts, infected areas have watersoaked appearance. Sometimes the spots merge to make large, straw-colored areas. When dew is on the grass, you can see cobwebby growth on the spots.

Pink patch, red thread (Corticum). Active in lawns from late fall through late spring. Causes yellowing discoloration of grass in spots 2 to 12 inches in diameter. Within those areas, look very closely or use a magnifying glass and you can see pinkish webbing on the lower part of the leaf blades and sometimes woven from leaf to leaf. Late fall feeding is the best control.

Snow mold (Typhula). Dirty white patches appear in the lawn, varying from almost white through shades of light tan to buff. Margins to the spots are rather distinct. Dead grass can be pulled up easily. It has been found in all seasons and almost all places, but is quite common in early spring after snow melts.

Fusarium patch or pink snow mold. Tan to dark brown patches appear in the fall, sometimes in spring, seldom in summer unless it is cool and moist. The margins on the patches are rather indefinite.

How a fungicide works

Nobody really knows for sure exactly how turf fungicides work, but this explanation offered by the pathologists and chemists seems quite plausible: The chemicals coat the surfaces of the above-ground parts of the grasses in a sort of protective armor. Then, when the ubiquitous airborne or soilborne spores land on the grass surfaces, they find an unfavorable environment and they either do not germinate or the mycelium dies soon after germination.

If you apply a fungicide to a lawn after you see evidence of the disease, the chemicals have to do their job the hard way. The fungus mycelium is already inside the grass tissue. The blades that are dead, dying, or discolored cannot be saved by most fungicides.

However, if the infected lawn was healthy before the attack, new blades will grow from the roots and runners. Grass has an amazing vitality. Without any protection, these new blades might fast become infected from the older, diseased blades. Repeated applications of a fungicide applied to cure a fungus infection should protect the new shoots. In time, maybe as long as six weeks, green leaf blades (healthy) will begin to outnumber the shriveled leaf blades (infected), and the lawn will be on the way to recovery.

Applying a fungicide as a curative means dropping everything else. Prevention is much easier. As a curative, a fungicide must be put on every seven days (or as frequently as the label directions prescribe). At the same time, you must water carefully (not too much and not too little), and withhold fertilizer unless the fungicide label directions prescribe feedings during the treatment.

The summer and early fall malady that comes to western cool-season grass lawns every year has always gone away when the cool nights come along in autumn. Green grass begins to replace brown at that time. You never know then whether it was your late-summer treatments or the change of season that did the trick.

But don't gamble on the cool nights to save an infested lawn. Some years, infected lawns are so sick by fall that they never recover fully, and have to be reseeded in spots in spring, or dug up and completely replanted.

Timing for preventive application

Enough said about *cures*. Far much better to *prevent* the possibility of lawn disease infection before it happens. And since most diseases come on in summer, "before it happens" means in spring—start in the month of May. Four applications at 10-day to two-week intervals should render any lawn almost completely immune to disease attack. (Red thread and fusarium patch or pink snow mold come in late fall through late spring.)

Weak lawns are vulnerable. If your lawn has had midsummer trouble before and you are applying a broad spectrum fungicide as a preventive, don't let the lawn suffer from lack of water. Two of the chief suspects in the midsummer plague complex—curvularia and helminthosporium—are present most of the time, and go into action on weakened grass. Poor watering and lack of fertilizer when it was needed in spring make grass weak fast in early summer.

Check water penetration. See if soil is equally moist at all levels in the top foot; it should be. A mat of thatch—tightly interwoven dead grass growth between grass and the soil—can slow entry of water into soil. Dense soil can also slow entry of water, causing most of it to run off onto the sidewalk and down the street. Get rid of thatch in fall or spring with a vertical-cutting machine, available at some rental agencies. Correct compacted soil by aerating with a plugging tool that removes cores of soil.

Do not use household bleach. Chlorinated household bleach often cleans up a fungus infestation in a lawn. Some professional gardeners and garden consultants have recommended it. But the manufacturers of the product, themselves, would prefer that it not be used for this purpose. The end decomposition product of chlorinated household bleach in soil is common salt.

Fairy ring and other mushrooms

A toadstool or mushroom is the fruiting body of a type of fungus. The actual vegetative portion from which the mushroom grows is the mycelium, a filament-like underground growth. The mycelium feeds on organic matter. Sometimes, old pieces of wood, or clods of turf which were once turned beneath the soil under the grass, can support the mycelium.

Mushrooms sometimes grow in an expanding circle, called a fairy ring. The mycelium growth is always just beneath the ring of mushrooms. Sometimes this mycelium is so dense and tough that water and air cannot get through to the grass roots, and the grass either suffers temporarily or dies completely. However, the mycelium inside the circle deteriorates as the mushroom-mycelium circle expands, and in deteriorating it supplies nutrients to the grass roots. The grass inside a fairy ring is often greener than anywhere outside.

Actually, fairy ring growth may take place at any time of year, and its consequences are most serious when it takes place in summer. At that time the mycelium can keep water from reaching the grass roots.

Isolated mushrooms, or little shapeless colonies of mushrooms are strictly cool-season phenomena. Although they grow from a mycelium and feed on organic matter, the lawn damage is usually of little consequence. But they might be poisonous, and homeowners fear the possibility that a child or a pet might eat them. That's reason enough for action.

Any mushroom in a lawn should be picked as soon as you see it—before the cap opens up. When the cap opens, many spores are released, and the chance of more growth is greatly increased. Put the mushrooms in a paper bag, fold it up tight, and throw it in the garbage can.

It's next to impossible to get mycelium of any mushroom or toadstool out of the soil. It can be done with the all-out grass-killing sterilant methyl bromide, but the need is seldom that great.

Mercurial fungicides listed in the chart on page 68 will check the growth of underground mycelium for a season or so. Poke holes in the lawn around the mushroom infested area, at least 12 inches beyond the fairy ring margin. Holes should be at least four inches deep, and about six inches apart. Pour the fungicide down the holes. If you pull mushrooms out of the lawn, stem and all, pour the mercurial fungicide down the stem holes, too. Use label-recommended proportions.

Damping off, a disease of young seedlings

Shortly after germination, young grass seedlings suddenly wilt, lose stamina, look as if burned by acid. It's damping off, a fungus disease. Give infected areas extra water (contrary to instinct and usual recommendation for sick lawn), and treat with captan or mercurial fungicide. Reseed if necessary.

Moss in the lawn

A green moss among the grass blades usually indicates low soil fertility, too much moisture, and too much shade. Regular fertilizing may solve the problem.

Moss in the lawn under trees is usually the result of too much shade plus low fertility because of root competition. Apply 1½ to 2 times the usual amount of fertilizer to these areas.

In areas where soil is likely to be acid, a lime treatment combined with a fertilizer application may banish the moss. Apply 40 to 50 pounds of hydrated lime to each 1,000 square feet.

Other products and treatments that have effectively controlled moss in lawns:

A commercial lawn fungicide containing phenyl mercuric acetate and thiram.

Hydrated ferrous ammonium sulfate, applied according to label directions.

Copper sulfate, 5 ounces in 4 gallons of water per 1,000 square feet.

When moss growth is caused by water standing on the soil or in the top layer of soil, soil conditions obviously need improvement. Dig up the bad section in the spring, then mix in some soil conditioning material. Level the newly prepared soil in the old bad area so that it no longer will collect water; then reseed.

If poor drainage is the cause, you will be ahead of the game if you correct it once and for all, even if it means installing underground drain tiles.

In the Pacific Northwest we've seen chronically mossy spots on lawns on the shady north side of houses, fences, and walls, where nothing can be done to admit more sunlight. Frequently, the best plan is to remove the lawn in such spots and replace it with paving of some kind, or with ferns or other shade-loving plants.

PHYSICAL TROUBLES IN LAWNS

Sometimes there are physical or mechanical causes of poor performance in a part of a lawn. These conditions are usually of a permanent or repetitive nature and will cause trouble until you correct them (whereas a rainfall can end a drought condition or an insect or disease can just vanish). Here we check off many such possible physical causes of lawn troubles. But, first, we would ask you these important questions again: Have you fed your lawn lately? Are you watering it properly?

Check list of physical lawn troubles

☐ **Have you applied a chemical fertilizer or weed killer in the past week?** If this spot showed up since then, does its shape show any relation to the course you followed with the dispenser or spreader (streaks, square spots, half-moons)? This would be chemical burn and there isn't much you can do about it. Try watering the spot heavily to flush the excess chemicals out of the topsoil, if you wish. Otherwise, let nature take its course and this spot will soon turn green again.

☐ **Has this spot persisted through all the seasons for a year or so?** If so, get down on your knees and sight across it. Is the bad grass within a high or low spot? Either of these physical features can bother grass—too much water on a low spot or too little on a high spot. Fix the hill or dale by inserting a flat spade under the turf (2 or 3 inches beneath the surface) and lifting it out in sections. *If it's a low spot,* fill in under the lifted area with enough enriched, conditioned soil to bring the turf section up to grade. Water it well to adjust for the shock of digging. Roll or press the sections into place only if they appear very uneven. *If it's a high spot,* remove enough soil to bring the hump down to grade, replace the sod, and water it well.

☐ **Does water enter the soil, stand on the surface, or flow off?** Compaction by traffic, a build-up of thatch beneath the grass, or just plain soil contrariness can be responsible. Open the compacted area up to water with a soil corer or aerator. (See pages 72 and 73.)

☐ **Perhaps your sprinkler system or portable sprinkler isn't giving adequate water to the area.** Check the water dispersal. (See watering chapter.)

☐ **Are the bad spots in a shady place?** If the shade comes from trees, perhaps if you thin the branches out to let more light through, the grass will grow better. Feed a lawn under a tree at least three times a year to replace the nutrients taken by the trees. Some trees are moisture robbers—try watering the spot more than you do the rest of the lawn. In addition to the other measures, try cutting the grass higher under trees. Also look at the grass variety charts on pages 11 to 14. You will see that in both

VERTICAL MOWER. Revolving knives slice through grass and thatch to ground surface and comb out mat of dead material that prevents water from penetrating

POWER AERATOR. This machine is useful for aerating large lawn areas. It operates on the same principle as the foot aerator shown in the photograph below

cool-season and tropical grasses, there are some types that do much better in shade than others. If the lawn continues to fail in the shade, substitute a shady ground cover such as ajuga, helxine, or *Vinca minor*.

☐ **Does a female dog roam the premises?** She can be responsible for little dead spots often surrounded by a

ring of very green grass. Soak them well and they should come back eventually; if not, reseed.

☐ **The only remaining possibility is that something is wrong underground.** Use a soil corer or auger, a soil sampling tube, a crowbar or jack handle, or dig down with a spade to see what's the matter. If you find some debris below, remove it. If you find a hard clay layer, dig it out and replace with good soil, of the same texture as above and below. After you finish the operation, make a seedbed over the area, sow new grass seed on it and give this spot the care you would give a new lawn until it's up and growing fast.

How to aerate your lawn

Compacted soil can be opened by aerating tools that remove small cores of earth. For a few dollars, you can get a 2, 3, or 4-tube aerator that you push into the ground with your foot. For close to $50, you can get a small weighted mobile aerator, one on which the coring tubes are arranged on a wheel. All you do is push it back and forth. If you have a large area to contend with, you can rent or hire a machine-operated aerator (the kind used on

FOOT AERATOR. Simple foot-operated aerator has tubes through which plugs of sod and soil are removed

golf greens, football fields, and baseball diamonds) to come in and open up the compacted soil.

One trouble you will run into here is that the dirt may be so compacted that you can't get the aerator in more than about an inch. The only answer turf experts can give you is, "Be patient." Water the area slowly up to its capacity the day before. Aerate the area to whatever depth you can; run a sprinkler on it long and slow. After it has dried enough to lose all stickiness, come back and try again. The first pass with the aerator will have opened the ground so water can make the soil soft enough.

You can just aerate a compacted spot and leave the holes open. Grass roots will fill it. But, since you know your soil is inclined to pack, you can make the job pay off by raking into the areas a top-dressing that contains 50 to 100 per cent fine sand. If your soil isn't too clayey, let the plugged cores lay on the ground until they can be crumbled by dragging a mat over them. Mix fine sand with the crumbled cores and brush or rake the mixture into the holes.

The practice of driving a fork into the ground instead of an aerating tool is not recommended. It is liable to make the condition worse by compacting the soil at each point where the tines enter.

There are cures for run-off spots on existing lawns short of ripping up your lawn and starting all over. For one thing, wetting agents, now sold at garden supply stores, may help, if applied consistently. Also there is the bottled garden chemical described on labels as "calcium polysulfide." It has many garden uses; fundamentally, it is a fungicide for mildew and peach leaf curl control. It is also used for reclamation of excess-sodium soils. Chemically, it is liquid gypsum. You can put it in solution and soak it into hard spots (in alkaline soil) and often get noticeable results. In soils where there is no excess sodium for it to act on, it may be the wetting agent contained (and so stated on the label) that is doing the job.

Dry gypsum on existing lawns has less effect than when worked into the soil. Best idea is to use gypsum in a top-dressing and rake it into a hard area that you have opened with an aerating tool.

Thatch can make water run off, too

A lawn may build up a dead-looking layer of thatch—old grass and stolons—between the soil surface and the green grass blades above. Often this thatch will stop downward movement of water. Two kinds of thatch will cause trouble: (1) a layer of matted clippings made by mowing tall grass without a grass-catcher; (2) a thicker, more springy layer of old stems and stolons beneath the green grass blades, caused by the natural growth pattern of the grass mixture.

You can usually scratch matted clippings out with a rake. Thereafter, prevent its formation by using a grass-catcher, by mowing often enough so that the clippings are not longer than ¼ to ½ inch, or by cross-mowing to chop up the cuttings into shorter lengths. Certain types of rotary mowers chop the clippings into short lengths.

SOIL SAMPLER TUBE helps you to find where compaction occurs. Two photographs at right show untreated soil (water penetrates only a few inches), and treated soil. Better water penetration promotes deeper rooting

Sometimes, a too-frequent fertilizing schedule will build up thatch, especially in the east.

Opening up a thatch of interwoven stolons and stems can be difficult. The mat may be 1½ to 2 inches thick, with the texture of a horsehair mattress. A machine especially designed to comb out this kind of thatch is manufactured and available at most equipment rental places.

Many revolving vertical knives slice down through the grass and the thatch to the ground surface. They leave enough rooted grass plants so the lawn can recuperate fast. But they also comb out great quantities of dead material and once again open up the stolon mat so water can get into the soil. Use this machine to cure a lawn that has grown lumpy. Another power driven machine combines the combing and thatch removal with the sweeper shown on page 47.

Gophers and moles

The success or failure of a campaign to rid your lawn and garden of these pests often depends more upon perseverance than on the type of control you use. The three controls used most frequently are the trap, poison, and gas.

Gophers are slipshod excavators. Their mounds are irregular, often fan-shaped, with the hole located where the handle of the fan would be. The hole is usually plugged up, but still discernible.

Moles throw up round, conical mounds, composed of loose chunks of earth from their main runs. They force plugs of earth up to the surface, but they do not open the tunnel. The ridges you see in your lawn where soil has been raised are hunting paths and are seldom used more than once.

Traps. Traps have two outstanding advantages over poison or gas; you actually see the dead gopher or mole, and trapping is the safest method of control. The Maca-bee trap is considered to be the most successful for gophers. The lateral-jawed type is most effective for moles.

Poison bait. Although less sure than trapping, poison bait is the control preferred by many people because it requires less digging. Also, you can poison large areas faster by using bait than by trapping. Pieces of root vegetables or dried prunes dusted with powdered strychnine are very effective in poisoning gophers. For moles, some of the dried fruit, vegetable, and grain baits with thallium sulfate as the toxic agent have proved highly successful.

Gas. Under certain conditions (damp, tight soil, limited runway system), gas either destroys gophers and moles or causes them to move out. Gas is more expensive to use than bait. Gases that have been used on gophers and moles include calcium cyanide, methyl bromide, carbon monoxide, and carbon disulphide.

LAWN RESEEDING

An existing lawn should be reseeded only if the trouble that caused the need for renovation isn't a basic fault. If there is a basic trouble, renovating will probably only bring about the same headaches at the same time next year.

But if you have lost a portion of a lawn or even an entire lawn from an outside factor that you can be sure of—such as a lawn moth infestation, a disease attack, or a long drought—and if the lawn is still approximately as level and smooth as you want it, reseed, as follows:

1. Mow the remnants of the old lawn thoroughly.

2. Rake up all the clippings.

3. With a hard steel rake, scrape away at the old turf surface. Pull up runners, rough up the surface without really breaking it up into clods.

4. Go over the lawn again with the mower set as low as possible to cut off the runners you have exposed and pull any weeds that might remain.

5. Rake again.

6. If there are any obvious low spots, fill them in with a mixture of compost and soil, or any mixture that you would use to germinate seeds.

7. Cut off the humps that might show up, and rake and treat the scalped soil as deeply as the surrounding area.

8. If there are hard spots, aerate them as outlined on page 72. If a serious weed problem is the reason for renovating the lawn, treat it at this point with Vapam or dig up the old turf and treat with calcium cyanamide. Because these chemicals kill grass as well as weeds, you must start over and sow new grass. (See weed chapter.)

9. Apply fertilizer as for a new lawn.

10. Scatter seed over the sparse spots and cover them with a seedbed mulch.

11. Water as deeply as you can right at the start— without washing out the filled areas and the seeds.

12. Keep the newly planted patches from drying out for two weeks or so until the new grass is firmly established. It is at this point where reseeding programs frequently fail. It is much easier to forget to water a little reseeded patch the size of a plate than it is to forget to water a new lawn.

Winter Grass for Bermuda Lawns

Come September and October, some homeowners in a southerly belt below the line extending from Richmond, Virginia, to Santa Barbara, California (mapped on page 8), have for generations been sowing "winter grass" in their Bermuda grass lawns.

The seed they sow germinates and grows up in late fall to make green grass in winter—green that will hide the winter-browned Bermuda grass. Then, in spring, when the heat comes on, the winter grass begins to weaken and the Bermuda comes back into its own again.

The usual September-October procedure is as follows: Mow the old lawn as closely as possible. Rake up the clippings with a hard steel rake (there are some available called Bermuda grass rakes). Rake hard enough to scrape at the old turf beneath, pulling up loose runners and roughing up the surface. Then, mow the area again to cut off the runners you exposed in the raking. Pull any weeds that remain. Rake the lawn again.

At this time you can spread some sand-and-peat moss mixture in low spots to bring them up to grade. If necessary, slice off the tops of any humps that show up. Next, scatter the seed over the lawn. Rate of seeding should be higher than labels recommend for new lawns (use as much as 20 to 50 pounds of rye grass seed per 1,000 square feet). Cover the seed with a light mulch of dampened peat moss or old manure. Water to soak the mulch and seeds, and from then on treat the renovated lawn just as if it were a new lawn—chiefly a matter of watering carefully until the new grass is well established.

There are numerous other ways of doing it—variations on the main theme, you might say. Here is a fairly common version on the simpler side: Cut the lawn as short as possible (about ½ inch). Then rake off the heaviest of the cut grass, sow the annual rye grass, and mow once more after sowing. Leave all the clippings on the lawn after the second mowing to provide the mulch that seeds need for temporary cover. After sowing, begin a regular new-lawn watering program. Put on a high-nitrogen fertilizer after grass has started.

Annual rye grasses, sold at all nurseries in Bermuda country, is far and away the most common type used as a winter grass. Theoretically, all the annual rye dies out by early summer, letting the Bermuda take over. However, patches may remain throughout the summer.

Red fescues serve well. Although more expensive than annual rye, they aren't as long lasting and competitive. Sow 10 to 20 pounds per 1,000 square feet.

Bent grass has proved satisfactory in many cases. The texture and blade size of the bents and Bermudas are similar enough to make a uniform-appearing turf. Cutting heights are the same. The bent that lives through the summer will be less obvious than the annual rye that might live through. Bents get more insects and diseases than the Bermuda and need more summer watering. In total, if you want to keep a continual bent-Bermuda combination, it will mean more maintenance effort.

Various turf dyes are available which give dormant grass lawns a presentable green color.

RENOVATING WITH MACHINES

The methods described above of sowing seed for winter color work best if you have cut your Bermuda lawn as low as possible all summer. Mowing too high allows Bermuda to develop a thatch, sometimes several inches deep, of criss-crossed runners. Sometimes such a thatch gets deep enough that the regular means of making ready for annual rye for winter won't work. In that case, use of a renovating machine is in order.

Renovating with a machine will correct a thatch for the time being. But, as you might imagine, it has a definitely weakening effect on grass—even on the mighty Bermuda. A renovated Bermuda lawn may come back too slowly in spring, allowing crabgrass and other weeds to get a foothold when the warm days of spring and early summer begin to eliminate the winter grass. Southwest turf experts recommend that machine renovating be done not more than once every three years.

The Dichondra Lawn

Dichondra is a soft, green, ground-hugging, broad-leafed plant—not a grass. In the milder parts of California and Arizona it is used quite widely as lawn. But it need not be limited to this part of the West. It could probably be grown as a lawn almost anywhere in the Bermuda grass belt (mapped on page 8). It grows in the southeastern states now and some few people there have maintained it as a lawn. But the Agricultural Extension Services in several southern states have listed dichondra —a member of the bindweed family—under "weeds," where it appears by the name ponyfoot.

Dichondra has some definite advantages as a turf plant (and, like grasses, some disadvantages, too). Watching it boom in popularity in California during the 1950's made us believe that someday it may be taken for granted as a turf plant wherever average winter temperatures don't drop below 25°. Dichondra does not grow well in California's extreme coastal areas subject to fog. Environment there favors grasses.

WHEN TO PLANT DICHONDRA

Sow the seed any time between March 1 and October 15. Although dichondra germinates fastest in midsummer, people have had trouble with it then because it is difficult to keep the new seedlings moist enough. Seed sown in March, April, or May gets firmly enough established by summer to withstand the moisture loss on hot summer days.

In winter and early spring, the ground is too cold to germinate the seeds. They will just sit there until spring and then begin to sprout. Meanwhile, you have to battle weeds that sprout in the cold ground.

BEST SOIL FOR DICHONDRA

Recent experience has shown that dichondra definitely grows better in light, sandy loam soil because water can penetrate better, roots grow deeper, summer water-stress is less. That, of course, is also true of a grass lawn.

Heavy clays or adobes should have peat moss, ground bark, or sawdust plus nitrogen (see instructions on page 17) dug uniformly and thoroughly into the top 6 inches before dichondra is planted in it.

In March, April, or May, dichondra seed needs no mulching. Just rake the seed gently to bring it into contact with the soil surface, and roll it with a light roller.

If you sow in summer, apply a covering of damp peat moss no deeper than 3/8 inch. Keep the seedbed moist, either way. At time of seeding, apply a complete fertilizer to the seedbed. Follow the label's instructions for new lawns.

HOW MUCH SEED TO BUY

In dichondra's early days, almost everyone—including packagers of the seed—erred in the direction of recommending too little seed per square foot. One ounce of seed to 1,000 square feet would make a dichondra lawn in time, but it would take several years for such a thin spreading to make a solid green lawn. In recent years, labels have recommended much more seed per square foot. Yes, it costs more, but for the extra cost, you get a lawn faster and will save yourself a great deal of weeding in bare spots.

Two pounds (32 ounces) of dichondra seed to 1,000 square feet, sown in March to May, will give you a beautiful lawn in 5 weeks. One pound to 1,000 feet will do it in 6 or 7 weeks. The more you stretch the seed, the longer you have to wait—it's as simple as that. And the longer you wait, the more opportunity there is for weeds to come up in the growing lawn.

MATURE DICHONDRA RESEEDS IN MAY

Since dichondra has become widespread, gardeners in many Western communities have found the plant coming up as a volunteer in their grass lawns. Many have encouraged the dichondra by mowing the mixed lawns just above the dichondra leaves, thereby helping the dichondra to crowd out the grass. Those who want to keep their grass lawns pure should kill the dichondra with 2,4-D. Don't wait too long or the treatment will leave a thin stand of grass.

DICHONDRA, the soft, green, ground-hugging, broad-leafed plant that is used quite widely as a lawn in California and Arizona. Notice the typical irregularly rounded leaves. At the right is ground cover juniper

"But," people ask, "how did we get dichondra without planting it?" It's easy to understand how birds can spread pyracantha and California pepper but you can't see any seeds on dichondra for the birds to eat.

The birds know where to find the seeds. In May, dichondra plants set seeds *underneath* the leaves. You may never even know they are there, but the birds go in and get them. The next thing you know, people on the next block have a patch of dichondra in their blue grass lawn.

Dichondra spreads as much by reseeding as it does by the runners that grow underground. Water will carry the seeds laterally for small distances. Because of this natural seeding, dichondra lawns that are sparse in spring will sometimes suddenly burgeon and spread during the early summer months.

WHAT ABOUT DICHONDRA IN MIXES?

The scheme of sowing dichondra with white Dutch clover was thought of some years ago when dichondra was priced like diamonds. Another old notion of sowing a mixture of dichondra and a grass such as perennial rye has been completely forsaken. Straight dichondra simply needs no nurse crop, not if it's sown in spring on a well-prepared soil, watered well, and fed frequently. The nurse crop turns out to be more nuisance than benefit.

An old argument for using clover with dichondra was that the clover would, in theory, come up before the di-chondra and offer shade and protection. Then, in later seasons, the nitrifying nodules on the clover roots would simply supply nitrogen to the dichondra and thereby make the dichondra grow stronger.

Instead, what often happened was that you'd get more clover than dichondra—permanently. Left unmowed, clover grows to about 6 or 7 inches, dichondra grows only about 3 inches. Frequently the clover would shade the dichondra out of existence. In addition, clover requires no nitrogen, dichondra requires it. If you skip a feeding (which is easy to do when you see the lawn green with clover), clover takes over at dichondra's expense.

Some seed companies recommend the clover-dichondra mix if you want to sow in late fall or midwinter (the latter is not a wise time to sow any kind of lawn). If you use the mix and want to keep the two plants at a balance or give the dichondra the upper hand, mow to dichondra leaf height frequently and feed regularly as described below.

PLUG PLANTING

Starting a dichondra lawn from flats was at one time the only method used.

The criticism that "plug planting creates a lumpy surface" can often be attributed to improper techniques. Seed planting can also create a lumpy surface if your soil is not properly leveled.

By nature, dichondra makes a smooth surface, and

when properly grown and cared for, it should give you an even surface.

Plug planting is practical if you desire an immediate effect or if the areas are small like those between stepping stones or on banks and slopes. Carefully insert the plug so that the top is level with the ground, and tamp it in patiently and gently. This care will make the difference between a smooth or lumpy planting.

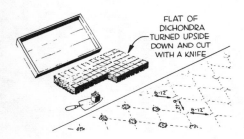

Plugs should be no smaller than 1 inch square—preferably 2 inches square or larger. The larger the plug, the quicker the dichondra responds to transplanting. To get the strips or plugs, turn the flat over on a level surface and cut through the soil with a knife or saw. Or

you can rent or buy a dichondra transplanter from your nurseryman. This instrument, which works like a big cooky cutter, will not only cut the dichondra plugs but will also make identically sized holes in your planting area.

In placing plugs into soil, make sure that runners at the top of the plug are at soil level or just below. Then, press each plug down hard. Offset planting (see sketch) provides a more even distribution and a quicker covering than a square pattern. Place plugs 6 to 12 inches apart.

FREQUENT MILD FEEDINGS BEST

As you may have gathered by now, dichondra is a full-draft plant. Far from low maintenance or no maintenance, it needs as much care as a grass lawn if it's to look nice at all times. Regular watering is its first important need, including long waterings in summer to make the roots grow deep. Along with the careful watering, dichondra needs a continual supply of nutrients.

Dichondra seems to respond more noticeably than grass to the frequent-mild-feeding type of schedule. Try this: Feed with the lightest feeding recommendation on a fertilizer's label, once every 2 to 4 weeks.

ABOUT MOWING AND LEAF SIZE

How tall, lush, and loose dichondra grows depends on three things: the use it gets, including your mowing habits; the fertility of its soil; the amount of shade.

The more traffic dichondra gets, the smaller, tighter, and more compact the leaves grow. Frequent low mowing has the same effect.

At *Sunset's* original building in Menlo Park, in a garden bed since remodeled, we planted some dichondra in a bed under an olive tree. It was fed frequently, got considerable shade, and nobody walked on it. This dichondra grew 6 inches high, as lush as leaf lettuce—between mowings. The same dichondra grew into the cracks between adobe bricks in the adjoining sun-baked patio. There, under the daily footsteps of several hundred people, it hugged the ground. The little ¼-inch-diameter leaves overlapped tightly.

On regularly used badminton courts and other places that get regular heavy traffic, dichondra grows as it grew in *Sunset's* patio—low and tight. Under such conditions, mowing is needed much less than in seldom-used lawns. Wherever traffic is light, feeding is ample or heavy, and the lawn is partially shaded, you should mow frequently if you want even texture. Otherwise, your occasional mowing will give a very noticeable scalped look for a few weeks.

DICHONDRA AND SEDUM cover the ground around these large concrete pads which lead the visitor to the front door. Design: Eckbo, Royston, and Williams

PANELS OF DICHONDRA divide the patio sections of gravel and concrete. The dichondra adds color and texture to the patio area and relieves the severity of the grid pattern. Design: Schuyler Reed Hafely

Big, lush-growing dichondra has given rise to a myth that you can buy "big-leafed dichondra" or "little-leafed dichondra." There is no such distinction on the West Coast. There is a separate species or variety with extra big leaves grown in the southern United States, but all other dichondra is the same plant. Conditions make the difference.

WEED CONTROL

The best weed control is simply to keep your dichondra lawn growing so luxuriantly that yellow oxalis, Bermuda grass, annual bluegrass *(Poa annua),* crabgrass, or nutgrass can never get in. But, should you fail and one of the outsiders appear in your dichondra, act fast to get it out. You can hand-pull an isolated weed. Do it before it spreads.

Several different weed killing compounds are used in products sold as broad-spectrum weed killers for selective weed control in dichondra lawns, usually mixed with fertilizer, too. Each one will kill certain weeds (or their germinating seeds) in a dichondra lawn without harming the dichondra—*if you follow the application directions to the letter!* Used carelessly or in too great quantities any one of these ingredients can kill the dichondra as well as the weeds upon which they are effective.

Here are the ingredient names; look for them in the "active ingredient" list on the labels (the products themselves have various trade names): monuron, neburon, diphenamid, azac, and betasan.

Monuron is marketed chiefly as an oxalis killer but it can also control most of the weeds upon which the other three are effective. Pound for pound, it is the one that must be used with greatest care (it has the greatest potential hazard).

Neburon controls yellow oxalis, chickweed, white clover, spurge, annual bluegrass, crabgrass, and other annual grasses.

Diphenamid controls almost the same group of weeds as neburon. It is not listed as effective on yellow oxalis.

Azac controls crabgrass.

Betasan kills crabgrass, annual bluegrass, and a number of difficult broad leafed weeds.

These weeds are described, and some of them pictured, in the weed control chapter on pages 49 to 59.

LAWNS OF DICHONDRA AND BERMUDA GRASS

Most California lawns are mixes of dichondra and grass. One of the most common stands is a Bermuda grass-dichondra blend. Usually, one of the two members came into the lawn as a volunteer. There is no selective weed killer that will satisfactorily kill Bermuda in a Bermuda-

DICHONDRA ADAPTS ITSELF very well to close-quarter situations like the one shown here. It stays flat and smooth, requires very little mowing and clipping

DICHONDRA NEAR POOL area provides a cool, green look that is restful contrast to hard white of concrete decking around pool. Design: W. Bennet Covert

dichondra lawn without killing the dichondra too.

However, dichondra is compatible with Bermuda. You can keep the two together as a presentable lawn. Or you can encourage the dichondra at the expense of the Bermuda.

Dichondra has a longer growing period than Bermuda. Dichondra starts growing in mid-February to early March in Southern California, and mid-March to early April in Northern California and Arizona. Bermuda comes out of winter dormancy about a month or two after dichondra. In the fall, Bermuda enters dormancy earlier than dichondra.

You can take advantage of these two growing cycles and establish an essentially pure dichondra lawn. Bermuda will be present but in the background. Here are the steps in achieving this aim:

(1) Fertilize the lawn in late January or early February. This makes food available to dichondra when it is coming out of dormancy.

(2) Feed the lawn regularly on a monthly or bi-monthly basis from spring through fall.

(3) Mow at 1½ inches. This high cut will shade some of the Bermuda and Bermuda cannot thrive in shade.

(4) Water regularly when it is not raining.

The Bermuda grass will make its biggest bid for competition in mid-summer. Then it will go into dormancy in the fall—and the continued feeding at this time will encourage the dichondra but not the Bermuda.

THE INSECTS THAT LIKE DICHONDRA

There has been little change over the years in the array of insects that eat dichondra. The controls available today are somewhat more effective.

Cutworms have been on the increase every year. You have a choice between sevin, dibrom, or diazinon. There is a dichondra fertilizer available that has sevin in it, enough to kill cutworms or lawn moths. Cutworms chew the dichondra at its base, make little holes through the turf. A bad attack can come on in just two or three days.

Lucerne moth larvae hatch from eggs laid by fawn-colored moths that flit around in daytime. The larvae are similar to but larger than sod webworms (discussed under lawn moth on page 66). Their feeding puts penny-sized pockmarks in otherwise evenly-textured dichondra lawns. Control with sevin.

Red spider sometimes builds up heavily for any of these reasons: after a DDT application; an abundance

DICHONDRA forms a beautiful, green, pleasantly textured carpet when grown under the right conditions, and for this reason has become increasingly popular in some areas as a substitute for the lawn grasses

of shade; if dichondra is allowed to grow tall and leggy; if there is a host plant nearby such as citrus. Red spiders yellow the leaves and stems. Control by treating with tedion, malathion, aramite, or kelthane.

Gnats may come into a dichondra lawn that has been fed with sewage sludge fertilizer or steer manure. The gnats lay eggs in the organic matter and become more of a nuisance than a dichondra pest. Spray with malathion.

Slugs and snails feed on dichondra. Best controls are the liquid metaldehyde slug and snail sprays. Make up a solution and pour it on the dichondra through a sprinkling can.

Nematodes are one of the most serious pests. We save them until last; we hope your dichondra never gets them. A nematode is an invisible eel-like animal that parasitizes roots, in this case. It causes little nodules to appear on the roots. The above-ground symptoms that show in the late winter and early spring months are a gradual decline in fullness, a yellowing, a bareness.

Nematodes may spread with dichondra sold in flats.

The use of nematicide such as DD and Telone on dichondra has not been very satisfactory. At best, it reduces the nematodes' activity for only about a year. If nematodes have the upper hand in your dichondra lawn, the best plan is to scrape off the dichondra, cultivate the soil thoroughly, treat it with Vapam or methyl bromide, and replant in a month or six weeks.

FUNGUS DISEASE

Dichondra lawns suffer from fungus disease some years.

Symptoms: yellowing, browning, and dying out in half-moon shapes, circles, or small spots in July and August. Black dots like radish seeds appear on infected plants. This is the sugar beet fungus (*Sclerotium rolfsii*). Two or three treatments with captan, PCNB, or a mercurial fungicide can stop the spread of the disease. The diseased spot should be replaced with plugs of live dichondra.

Symptoms: spots on the leaves in late spring. This is caused by several species of fungus and it is fairly easy to control with any turf fungicide.

THE BRIGHTER SIDE

Remember that you are reading through an exhaustive discussion of all things that can happen to dichondra. No dichondra lawn will suffer all of these maladies. All told, dichondra is as robust as grass—a little more so in some situations. For instance, the summer fungus that bothers bent and fescue lawns has never, to our knowledge, damaged a dichondra lawn.

Your Choices in Ground Covers

In many gardens there are places which need some kind of living carpet but where, for one reason or another, grass won't do the trick. Maybe you want to get away from mowing. Or you want something that takes less watering. Or you want one garden surface to look a little lusher and have a softer texture or deeper pile or nap, or a deeper shade of green. Or you may want a seasonal sea of color, and many ground covers will give you this.

The plants that are called ground covers will fill these needs. In fact, they are being grown more and more to meet such needs in some parts of the country. In the newer sections of Los Angeles you see far more front gardens carpeted with Algerian ivy, ivy geranium, bronze ajuga, or wild strawberry now than you see planted in lawn. Why the swing to ground covers there? It is partly just because they are in vogue nowadays, partly because the sloping banks are easier to maintain in ground cover than in lawn.

Do not kid yourself that ground covers are necessarily low-maintenance plants. Some of them are, of course, although they may be more difficult to establish than lawn. But any gardener who wants his ground cover planting to look uniform, dense, and healthy the year around will need to weed, feed, and water. As with any other kind of planting, ground covers respond noticeably to regular maintenance.

On the following pages we examine the performance and needs of plants that are in the nursery trade and can be grown as living carpets. The charts that begin on page 104 tell you quickly how hardy each plant is (whether or not it will grow in your climate), what some of its uses are, and what kind of exposure and soil it will tolerate. The written descriptions that follow describe the different plants. Less than half a dozen of the plants are truly lawn substitutes that you can walk on.

Certain vines such as gelsemium, Boston ivy, and Virginia creeper will ramble over the ground if given vertical support, and hence can be classed as ground covers.

AARON'S BEARD. See *Hypericum calycinum*.

ACHILLEA TOMENTOSA. WOOLLY YARROW. A flat mat of fernlike, dark green, woolly leaves highlighted by flat clusters of golden yellow flowers on 6 to 10-inch-high stems. It blooms by nature in May to mid-September, but you can prolong the bloom if you shear off flowers as they fade. Space plants 6 to 12 inches apart.

AEGOPODIUM PODOGRARIA. GOUT WEED, BISHOP'S WEED. A very vigorous (occasionally weed-like) ground cover that will grow under almost any conditions. It's widely used in eastern United States; seldom seen in the West.

The many dark green divided leaves make a low (6-inch), dense mass. There's a form with green and white leaves. With both types, foliage dies to the ground every winter. In the spring the new growth comes from creeping rootstocks. If you wish to keep this plant low, you can mow it with a lawn mower two or three times a year.

Goutweed is seldom sold in nurseries. Most people acquire it by getting divisions from friend's gardens.

AFRICAN DAISY, trailing. See *Osteospermum fruticosum*.

AJUGA. CARPET BUGLE. Rosettes or clumps of lustrous leaves form a thick evergreen carpet from a flat mat to a 6-inch height depending on the kind. Small flowers, in spikes, bloom from early spring to early summer.

A. reptans. A flat carpet of dark green leaves that grows to 2 inches high. Blue flowers in spikes 4 to 6 inches high. Forms with dark purple or bronze foliage, leaves variegated with yellow, and white flowered forms are available.

Two selected forms—the 'Giant' ajuga and 'Jungle' ajuga—have larger leaves than the species and make a higher more undulating ground cover. 'Jungle' ajuga has the largest leaves and the clumps grow to 6 inches high, with the flower spikes 6 inches higher.

A. reptans and its green forms are a good green color from early spring to first frost. Then they turn bronzy to red.

Start from rooted creeping branches, divisions, or flat-grown plants. Transplants best in spring or early fall. Plant 6 to 12 inches apart.

Feed in early spring, late summer. After bloom, trim or mow off old flower spikes. Water every week or 10 days during

AJUGA REPTANS
(Carpet bugle)

summer—more frequently in very hot or sunny locations. Keep fallen leaves raked off, or brush off with broom. Ajugas ultimately make such a tight cover that weeds can't compete. Occasionally yellow oxalis may get into the flat-growing ajuga cover.

ANDROMEDA POLIFOLIA. Bog rosemary. Low evergreen shrub to 1 foot high that spreads by creeping rootstocks. Leaves, to 1½ inches long, are green above, grayish beneath. Small white to pinkish flowers in clusters of 5 or 6 at the ends of the branches. The varieties 'Nana' and 'Nana Compacta' are lower growing and more compact.

Start by layers, from seed sown in finely ground peat moss, or softwood cuttings in late June. Plants are also available in gallon cans. Plant 1½ to 2 ft. apart.

Needs adequate moisture and acid soil to thrive

ANGEL'S TEARS. See *Helxine soleirolii.*

ANTHEMIS NOBILIS. Chamomile. Perennial evergreen herb that grows 3 to 6 inches high or more. Light bright green, finely cut leaves are aromatic; send out strong fragrance when stepped on. Most commonly grown form has summer-blooming flowers that look like small yellow buttons; but some forms have flowers like small daisies.

Plant divisions 12 inches apart. Requires mowing or shearing back to keep from becoming rangy. Weeds not problem after well established on properly prepared beds.

ARABIS CAUCASICA (*A. albida*). Wall rockcress. Evergreen gray-foliaged mats to 6 inches high. White ½-inch flowers almost cover the plant in early spring. Variety 'Variegata' has gray leaves with pale yellow margins.

Start from cuttings or from flats or gallon cans. Set plants 8 inches apart. Or sow seeds in early spring or fall. Needs shade in hot dry areas. Drought resistant; won't grow well in soggy soil. For compact plants cut half back after blooming.

ARCTOSTAPHYLOS UVA-URSI. Kinnikinnick, Bearberry. Prostrate evergreen shrub that eventually spreads to 15 feet. Reddish brown branches are thickly clothed with bright green, lustrous, 1-inch leaves that take on reddish or bronzy tints in winter. Small, bell-like, white or pinkish flowers in March to May are followed by small bright red or pinkish, apple-like fruits.

Set out plants from gallon containers. Since plants spread slowly, it is best to plant them 3 feet apart. Slowness to cover also poses a weed problem. Mulch with peat moss or sawdust to discourage weeds and keep soil moist for root expansion. Needs perfect drainage.

It is drought resistant, but needs some summer watering. In some parts of California, too much heat makes leaf tips turn brown.

ARENARIA. Two species in this genus are adaptable for ground cover use. They are low and carpet the ground with dense mats of foliage. Both have small white flowers in late spring and summer.

A. balearica. Corsican sandwort. Makes a dense mat (to three inches high) of oval, glossy leaves. Well suited to planting between stepping stones and in other limited areas. It grows best in the shade with lots of water.

A. verna caespitosa. Irish moss. Dense moss-like, evergreen mat of bright green foliage; cold weather will tend to lighten

ARCTOSTAPHYLOS UVA-URSI
(Kinnikinnick)

ARENARIA VERNA CAESPITOSA
FESTUCA OVINA 'GLAUCA' (rear)

color, even turn it silvery green in severe winter.

Plant plugs of Irish moss (from established plantings or from flats) 6 inches apart. Needs more frequent watering than a lawn. Preferably, feed with slow acting fertilizer. Crowds and becomes lumpy unless thinned by cutting out narrow strips. Initially, planting may look unsightly with weeds such as annual bluegrass, but it allows no weeds after it becomes well established.

ARMERIA MARITIMA. COMMON THRIFT. Evergreen tufted mounds that spread to 1 foot, with 6-inch-long, stiff, grass-like leaves. Small white to rose-pink flowers in compact clusters at the tops of 6 to 10-inch stalks. Bloom profusely in spring inland, longer on the coast; sometimes blooms intermittently throughout year.

Starting plants from divisions is least expensive but from flats will give faster coverage. Can be divided throughout the year but best in early spring or late fall. Plant 12 inches apart. Or sow seeds in spring and fall.

Shear flowers after bloom. Feed at least once a year. Use slow acting fertilizers if possible. In inland areas when planted in full sun, plants may brown out in spots; will need mulching and replanting. Eventually grows dense enough to discourage weeds.

ARTEMISIA SCHMIDTIANA. SILVER MOUND. Each plant forms domes of woolly, silver white foliage 10 to 12 inches across and up to 24 inches high. Prune the plants back severely each spring to keep them growing at a uniform height.

ASARUM CAUDATUM. WILD GINGER. Makes an evergreen, undulating, dark green sea of lush, 2 to 6-inch-broad, heart-shaped leaves to 7 inches high. Stems and roots have pungent odor of ginger when bruised. Springtime flowers are reddish brown with long tails, produced close to the ground under leaves.

Start plants from divisions or from gallon cans. Plant 12 to 15 inches apart. Requires moist soil.

ASPARAGUS SPRENGERI. SPRENGER ASPARAGUS. Graceful arching stems with slender, light green, needle-like, 1-inch leaves. Foliage usually becomes yellow-green in winter. Clusters of fragrant pinkish flowers in summer are followed by bright red fruits in winter.

Start plants from divisions of clumps, or from flats as seedling transplants. Also available in gallon containers; the root clumps can be divided. Plant 24 inches apart.

Feed several times a year for best appearance. Trim back after fruiting to keep plant more compact and more vigorous. Drought resistant. Growth habit is so open that weeds may be a problem. A mulch of sawdust or peat moss will help discourage weeds.

ASPERULA ODORATA. SWEET WOODRUFF. Attractive, low spreading, evergreen perennial reminiscent of deep shaded woods. Slender square stems 6 to 8 inches high, encircled every inch or so by whorls of eight aromatic leaves. Clusters of tiny white flowers show above green foliage in spring and summer.

In the right conditions (shade, rich soil, abundant moisture), sweet woodruff will spread rapidly and may become a pest.

Best use is in informal marginal areas for woodland effect. Space plants 18 to 24 inches apart.

BABY'S TEARS. See *Helxine soleirolii.*

BACCHARIS PILULARIS. DWARF COYOTE BUSH, DWARF CHAPARRAL BROOM. In California this prostrate, matting, very

ARMERIA MARITIMA
(Common thrift)

ASARUM CAUDATUM
(Wild ginger)

deep rooted, 2-foot-high native covers and holds slopes admirably. The kind of baccharis the nurseries sell lacks showy bloom. But the plant has many virtues. It takes any California climate; it grows in any soil (and the roots hold soil well); it needs little water. It's attractive all year (nitrogen fertilizer will increase greenness). Space plants 3 feet apart.

BAMBOO, dwarf. See *Sasa pygmaea.*

BEARBERRY. See *Arctostaphylos uva-ursi.*

BELLFLOWER. See *Campanula.*

BERGENIA CRASSIFOLIA *(Saxifraga crassifolia).* WINTER BLOOMING BERGENIA. Evergreen perennial that grows to 20 inches high from thick rootstocks. Forms clumps or colonies of large, thick, dark green, glossy leaves. Sturdy leafless stalks bear dense clusters of rose, lilac, or purple flowers in January and February.

Start plants from divisions or from gallon cans. Plant 1½ feet apart. Tolerates neglect but if not sheared will become leggy, overgrown, and unattractive. Seems to be a snail and slug haven (under the leaves). Best to divide clumps every two years (in fall) and discard old plants.

BIRD'S FOOT TREFOIL. See *Lotus corniculatus.*

BISHOP'S WEED. See *Aegopodium podograria.*

BLUE LEADWORT. See *Cerotostigma plumbaginoides.*

BOG ROSEMARY. See *Andromeda polifolia.*

BOUGAINVILLEA. In those subtropical areas where bougainvillea serves as a vine, the plant can also be used as a thorny ground cover. The purple-red to scarlet flowers don't mix well with other colors. In coastal Southern California bougainvillea

grows with no water once established. Don't remove nursery cans. Just slit the sides of the can and plant 6 feet apart.

BOX HUCKLEBERRY. See *Gaylussacia brachycera.*

BUNCHBERRY. See *Cornus canadensis.*

CALLUNA VULGARIS. SCOTCH HEATHER. There are many named varieties of this plant and they differ mostly in the color of their flowers from white, to pink, to red, and lilac. The varieties differ also in their height, varying from little dwarfs on which the flower spikes are 6 to 8 inches high to fair sized subshrubs with spikes 2 feet high. In all cases the flowers along the spikes are bell-shaped, about ¼-inch long.

Heather does best in poor soil; it should be acid and rather moist. In good garden soil the plants may become leggy.

Heather blooms from summer to fall. Clip it back hard in later winter and early spring so plants will grow back uniformly as a dense mat.

Space plants 12 to 18 inches apart.

CAMPANULA. BELLFLOWER. These perennials offer cup-shaped flowers of blue, violet, or white in different sizes in summer and fall. The foliage is dense and pleasing in spring and all during the flowering season, but in winter, typically, most of the ground cover forms lose a fair amount of foliage. As you see below, the four ground cover forms of campanula differ in manner of growing.

C. carpatica. CARPATHIAN OR TUSSOCK BELLFLOWER. This one makes leafy clumps or tussocks 9 to 18 inches high and as wide. Flowers grow on upright stems from these clumps. They are 1½ inches wide, violet to white.

ASPARAGUS SPRENGERI
(Sprenger asparagus)

CARISSA GRANDIFLORA (prostrate form)
(Natal plum)

C. elatines garganica *(C. garganica).* Forms tight mounds 3 to 6 inches high; blue star-shaped flowers cover the plants in summer and fall. Space the plants 6 to 12 inches apart.

C. portenschlagiana *(C. muralis).* Dalmatian bellflower. Grows as deep green, tufted foliage mats or mounds 4 to 7 inches high. Has violet blue, bell-like flowers in late spring to early summer. Set plants 8 inches apart.

C. poscharskyana. SERBIAN BELLFLOWER. This one also forms tufts but it spreads more than *C. elatines garganica.* Its spreading habit makes it the best of the campanulas for use as a ground cover. Flowers are lavender, ½ to 1 inch wide. Set the plants 6 to 12 inches apart.

CANDYTUFT, evergreen. See *Iberis sempervirens.*

CARISSA GRANDIFLORA. NATAL PLUM. Normally the species is a 5 to 7-foot-high shrub but there are three ground cover varieties—'Nana Compacta,' 'Prostrata,' and 'Tuttle.' Since there are so many variations even in these low growing forms, be sure to select plants that are prostrate, even in the gallon can.

Like the species, these low-growing Natal plums have very thorny branches. Foliage is dark green and glossy; in cold weather takes on a reddish purple tinge to the leaf margins. White, 2-inch flowers appear throughout the year and are followed by edible 1 to 2-inch-long, red, plum-like fruits.

Start plants from gallon cans set 3 feet apart. Since these plants are slow to start, regular feedings will encourage faster growth. Any vertical stems that appear should be trimmed off. Do not overwater in heavy soils. Weeds may be a problem, more so because the thorny nature of the plant makes weeding difficult.

CARMEL CREEPER. See *Ceanothus griseus horizontalis.*

CARPET BUGLE. See *Ajuga.*

CARPOBROTUS. See ice plant.

CEANOTHUS. Of the many ceanothus, there are several that have found favor in gardens as fast covering low ground covers that take little watering and little maintenance once they are established. They are especially adaptable to large scale plantings on steep banks.

C. gloriosus. POINT REYES CEANOTHUS. Low growing, dense mat, 4 to 24 inches high, spreading to 5 feet. Leaves are leathery, roundish, dark green, ½ to 1½ inches, with spiny-toothed margins. More rigid branches than other species. Lavender-blue springtime flowers in short stalked, rounded clusters.

C. griseus horizontalis. CARMEL CREEPER. Usually low and creeping but varies from 18 to 30 inches high with a 5 to 15-foot spread. Leaves are deep green, glossy, ovate, 1 to 2 inches. Dense clusters of blue flowers in March to May.

C. thyrsiflorus repens. CREEPING BLUE BLOSSOM. Prostrate plant with glossy dark green foliage. Blue flowers in compact 1 to 3-inch-long clusters in March to May.

Start ceanothus from gallon containers. Plant 3 feet apart for hillside plantings, 4 feet apart on level ground. Keep plants low by pinching back any upright growth that occurs. Once established little weeding will be necessary. Ceanothus are not long lived. Frequently they begin to die at 4 or 5 years. Replace the old, dead ones with new plants. Water standing around the crown of the plant is a common cause; level off rims of basins in fall to prevent water standing during long rainy periods.

CERASTIUM TOMENTOSUM. SNOW-IN-SUMMER. Low spreading, silvery-gray carpet; foliage good most of the year, less

CERASTIUM TOMENTOSUM
(Snow-in-summer)

CORNUS CANADENSIS
(Bunchberry)

gray in winter. Masses of white flowers in summer.

Start plants from divisions or from flats. Plant 18 inches apart in well-firmed soil. Or sow seeds. Seeds are the least expensive but flat-grown plants and rooted divisions will take over more rapidly.

In late spring or early summer, after bloom, trim with shears or rotary mower. Will come back quickly after shearing. Too much fertilizing causes rampant growth and long untidy runners. Too much shade and too much water also cause problems. Keep fallen leaves raked off. New plantings have normal weed problems, older none.

CERATOSTIGMA PLUMBAGINOIDES. BLUE LEADWORT. Dwarf, wiry-stemmed, evergreen perennial to 1 foot; spreads by underground stems which seldom root, but may get out of hand. Bronzy green foliage turns rich red-brown at first autumn frost. Clusters of intense blue flowers in early fall. Bedraggled for short time in winter, but fresh green leaves appear in early spring.

Start from divisions or gallon-can plants; set 18 to 24 inches apart. Cut back after bloom or in spring. Remove old crowns as they show signs of aging, replacing with rooted stems.

CHAMOMILE. See *Anthemis nobilis.*

CHAPARRAL BROOM, dwarf. See *Baccharis pilularis.*

CHECKERBERRY. See *Gaultheria procumbens.*

CINQUEFOIL. See *Potentilla verna.*

COMPTONIA PEREGRINA. SWEET FERN. Really not a fern at all, but a native shrub of eastern North America. This one performs well under a number of soil conditions, although acid soil seems to be best. It may grow as high as 4 feet, but as a ground

cover it's usually lower than that. The fern-like leaves are aromatic. You can plant it from seeds, divisions, or pieces lifted and transplanted as you would plant sod.

CONVALLARIA MAJALIS. LILY-OF-THE-VALLEY. This familiar perennial can serve as a good thick ground cover in half or full shade. The fragrant, waxy white, bell-like flowers on upright, 8-inch-high stems in late spring make the major display for this plant. By late summer, the oval leaves (8 inches long, 1 to 3 inches wide) often begin to look shabby and by winter the soil is bare.

Plant divisions (pips) 9 to 12 inches apart.

CONVOLVULUS MAURITANICUS. GROUND MORNING GLORY. Evergreen perennial that will grow 1 to 2 feet tall, and spread to 3 feet across. Soft gray-green foliage. Lavender-blue, 1 to 2-inch, funnel-shaped flowers from June to November.

Start plants from gallon containers; set them 3 feet apart. Sometimes available in 2½ or 3-inch pots. Plants have tendency to become woody but this can be prevented by a light trimming in late winter. Self-sow readily. Little watering needed after it is established. Somewhat open growth habit may allow weeds to creep in.

COMMON THRIFT. See *Armeria maritima.*

CORNUS CANADENSIS. BUNCHBERRY. A low-growing native of North America, it grows about 9 inches high and spreads by creeping roots. It holds its big 3-inch leaves horizontally to make a dense cover. White flowers in late spring are rather showy. They give way in late summer and fall to bright red berries in bunches. The plant dies down in the winter.

As a native plant, bunchberry makes the best show on the forest floor. However, under cultivation it seems to do well almost anywhere (including full-sun locations) except in climates of long summer drought.

Set plants or divisions about a foot apart.

CORONILLA VARIA. CROWN VETCH. This is a legume, a plant in the same family as alfalfa, sweet peas, and beans. It makes a vigorous ground-holding ground cover complete with large oval leaflets and pinkish white sweet pea-like flowers in summer. But the same rhizomes and intermeshed roots that hold the ground make this plant as difficult to contain or banish as Bermuda grass or quackgrass once it's established.

Sow seed on prepared soil or dig up divisions and plant them 6 feet apart.

CORSICAN SANDWORT. See *Arenaria balearica.*

COTONEASTER. So many plantings of the low-growing cotoneasters are made in situations where they are neglected that they're seldom seen at their best. Actually both the deciduous and evergreen forms are quality plants when used correctly.

C. adpressa. CREEPING COTONEASTER. Branches lie very close to the ground and often take root. Along these branches grow roundish leaves ¼ to ½ inch in diameter, and in fall, bright red berries about ¼ inch in diameter.

C. dammeri (*C. humifusa*). BEARBERRY COTONEASTER. Flat, evergreen, dense mat of long trailing branches that root as they spread. Rarely over 6 inches high. Glossy, bright green, 1-inch-long leaves, white flowers, scarlet berries.

C. horizontalis. ROCK COTONEASTER. Semi-evergreen to deciduous. Branches grow in neat, flat fans, horizontal to the ground,

but not dense enough to keep out weeds. Wide spreading but mounds to 3 feet high. Where winters are cold, scarlet berries color the branches to such an extent that you don't realize that the leaves are off.

C. microphylla. ROCKSPRAY COTONEASTER. Evergreen shrub spreading to 3 feet, sending out long runners that frequently root. Arching branchlets grow to 2 feet high. Leaves are small, about ⅓ inch, dark green above, gray beneath. Rosy red berries follow white flowers.

Two varieties are available: *C. m. thymifolia* has narrower leaves and 2 to 4 flowers in a cluster. *C. m. cochleata* is a prostrate form with spoon-shaped leaves. It reportedly has a much smoother habit of growth than *C. microphylla* and branches will not tangle up in the same way.

Start plants from gallon containers; set them 3 to 4 feet apart.

COTULA SQUALIDA. NEW ZEALAND BRASS BUTTONS. Evergreen perennial that grows only a few inches high but branches will creep 1 foot or more. The foliage is soft, hairy, fern-like, bronzy green. Flowers like yellow brass buttons (about ¼ inch diameter) in summer.

Start plants by divisions set 4 inches apart.

COYOTE BUSH, dwarf. See *Baccharis pilularis.*

CREEPING BLUE BLOSSOM. See *Ceanothus thrysiflorus repens.*

CREEPING SPEEDWELL. See *Veronica repens.*

CROWN VETCH. See *Coronilla varia.*

CRYOPHYTUM. See ice plant.

DELOSPERMA. See ice plant.

DIANTHUS. GARDEN PINK. Several of the pinks make interesting ground covers that form neat carpeting mounds of grass-like leaves—blue-green, green, or gray depending on the species or variety. Spring or summer flowers in pinks, reds, lavenders, and whites are usually spicily fragrant.

Start from divisions, or from flats. Set 6 to 9 inches apart. Can sow seed but it takes an extra 1 or 2 years for coverage. Shear severely after bloom to retain neatness and perhaps encourage a second bloom period. Keep well weeded until well established. If certain weedy grasses get in the planting, it's difficult to know which is the weed and which is the plant.

DROSANTHEMUM. See ice plant.

DUCHESNEA INDICA. INDIAN MOCK STRAWBERRY. Strawberry-like perennial trailer having bright green, long-stalked leaves, with 3 leaflets, on branches that root firmly along the ground. Small yellow flowers are followed by inedible red fruits which show well above the foliage.

Sow seeds or plant from flats. Set plants 12 to 18 inches apart. Grows so readily that it's apt to get out of hand.

EPIMEDIUM. Low trailing perennial plants that grow to about 9 inches high. The handsome leaves, divided into heart-shaped leaflets, are on long wiry stems. The new spring foliage often has warm bronze tones; sometimes take on bronze to reddish tints in winter. The leaves usually die down about Thanksgiving or Christmas.

Delicate sprays of small white, lilac, yellow, rose, or red flowers (depending on the kind you buy) in spring add to epimedium's charm. The blossoms last well when cut.

It's an especially good ground cover along paths, or massed under trees.

Plant divisions 12 inches apart in either fall or spring.

ERICA. HEATH. There are many species and varieties in this genus, both tall growing and ground cover types. All have small needle-like leaves and flowers in spike-like clusters. Below are two ground covering types. Start them from divisions of clumps in spring or fall. They tend to spread and become unsightly unless pruned annually to a clump.

DIANTHUS
(Garden pink)

CALLUNA VULGARIS (left)
(Scotch heather)

ERICA CILIARIS (right)
(Fringed heath)

E. carnea. SPRING HEATH. Evergreen low shrub to 8 to 15 inches, spreading to 2 to 3 feet wide. Spiky branches with dark green leaves; carmine flowers from January to May. There are several varieties that are often preferred to the species. They vary in height, foliage color, and/or flower color. Plant 3 feet apart.

E. ciliaris. FRINGED HEATH. Makes a shrubby mass to about 1 foot high. Rosy red flowers in 2 to 5-inch-long spikes bloom from summer to fall. Plant 1 foot apart.

ERIGERON KARVINSKIANUS *(E. mucronatus).* Graceful, rampantly trailing plant, with 1-inch, toothed or lobed leaves. White or pinkish, ¾-inch daisy flowers bloom freely from late spring to frost.

Start plants from divisions of clumps in spring or fall. Plant 1½ feet apart. Or sow seed. Will stand neglect. Cut back yearly after bloom to keep under control.

ERODIUM CHAMAEDRYOIDES. A perennial that forms low compact clumps of foliage about 6 inches high. It's a dainty looking ground cover with an interesting texture. The roundish leaves are about ⅓ inch long. For many months it bears ½-inch, cup-shaped, white flowers veined with pink. Variety 'Roseum' has pink flowers.

EUONYMUS FORTUNEI. WINTER CREEPER. An evergreen plant that trails on the ground or climbs by rootlets to 35 feet, with a 10-foot spread. Roundish, 1 to 2-inch leaves are dark green with toothed margins. Flowers are inconspicuous; seed capsules pinkish, but neither flowers or fruits are particularly ornamental— it's the foliage that counts.

Several varieties are more widely available than the species. *E. f.* 'Colorata' (purple-leaf winter creeper) has reddish and purple leaves in fall and winter. *E. f.* 'Kewensis' (Kew winter creeper) has the smallest leaves of any euonymus. It grows slowly, and is best used between stepping stones or rocks. *E. f. radicans* (common winter creeper) has smaller leaves than the species and they are more sharply toothed. *E. f.* 'Gracilis' has leaves variegated with white, yellow, or pink. *E. f.* 'Minima' is a creeping plant with small (½-inch) leaves. *E. f.* 'Vegeta' (Bigleaf winter creeper) has larger, rounder leaves than common winter creeper, more coarsely toothed, and more leathery.

Start plants from gallon containers. In some areas they are available in flats. Set plants 24 inches apart. Can also be grown from cuttings but it's slower. Slow to cover first year, and may have weed problem for several seasons. Once established there's little maintenance other than a little trimming for restraint.

FESTUCA OVINA 'Glauca' (F. 'Glauca') BLUE FESCUE. Blue-gray ornamental grass that grows in distinct tufts 4 to 10 inches high.

Plant divisions, flat-grown plants 6 to 12 inches apart, or

gallon-can plants 12 to 15 inches apart depending on effect desired. Cut back after flowering and at any time when plant begins to look shabby. Because this plant does not make a solid covering, weeds will be a continual problem. Will not tolerate wet, poorly drained soil. Depending on conditions, it may need replanting about every three years.

FOAM FLOWER. See *Tiarella cordifolia.*

FORGET-ME-NOT. See *Myosotis scorpioides.*

FRAGARIA CHILOENSIS. SAND STRAWBERRY, WILD STRAWBERRY. Low, compact, lush, evergreen mat of thick dark green foliage during growing season; takes on red tints during winter. Grows from 6 to 12 inches high but can be kept lower by mowing two or three times a year, leaving a ruff 2 inches high. Leaves are divided into 3 toothed leaflets. Large, 1-inch white flowers in early spring and bright red ¾-inch fruits in the fall. The hybrid variety 'No. 25' is the result of crossing the sand strawberry with a commercial variety, also does a superior job of carpeting and the fruit tastes especially good.

Can be planted from rooted stolons any time of the year but best in late spring or early summer. Flat-grown plants can be planted any time of the year. Set plants 12 inches apart for fast cover, or 18 inches apart if you are economical. Feed once a year after first mowing in late spring. Needs regular watering to look attractive. Needs regular mowing or cutting back to keep new growth coming and prevent high build-up of stems. In late summer, if leaves show yellowing, counteract with applications of iron sulfate. Ultimately cover may grow thick enough to crowd out weeds. Better on flat areas than on slopes.

GALAX APHYLLA. Shiny heart-shaped leaves 5 inches across turn a beautiful bronze color in fall. Whether green or bronze these leaves are handsome and are used in floral decorations. The plants grow about 6 inches high, have white flowers on long vertical, 2½-foot-high stems in July. Space plants 12 inches apart.

GAULTHERIA PROCUMBENS. WINTERGREEN, CHECKERBERRY. Low growing, spreading by creeping stems, the upright branches to 6 inches high. Oval, 2-inch-long, glossy leaves. Small, white, nodding flowers in late summer, and red berries during the winter months.

Plant from containers 12 inches apart. Keep weeded until well established.

GAYLUSSACIA BRACHYCERA. BOX HUCKLEBERRY. This hardy evergreen ground cover with lustrous leaves, is native to eastern United States, and takes the winters there in its stride. In late spring it shows a few white or pink flowers followed by blue berries in late summer. The plants spread slowly but with determination. Over a period of years one healthy plant can spread to cover a huge area.

GAZANIA. Low growing clumps that spread rapidly to form a solid mass of foliage. Leaves usually long and narrow, sometimes divided, dark green above, white woolly beneath. Abundant gaudy daisy flowers variously striped, banded, blotched or spotted on backgrounds of scarlet, wine, rose, white yellow, bronze, or orange. Bloom almost all year. Flowers close at night in shade, or on cloudy days.

G. rigens, the common orange gazania, has 1½-inch flowers, the orange rays varying to yellow, with a brown-black, white-eyed spot at the base.

G. pavonia has 3½-inch flowers, the orange-yellow rays with a white-ringed black spot at the base.

Many new gazanias are said to be hybrid descendants of this species and the dark-eyed yellow G. *rigens*. One such descendant is 'Copper King' which grows to about 1 foot. Its flowers include rich iridescent tones of yellow-orange, and brown with red-violet at the base of each ray, the base flecked with blue and buff. Blooms from October to April.

Start the above gazanias from divisions in midsummer, or from flats. Set 12 inches apart. At nurseries, you can also buy large mounded plants ready to give you a solid cover of flowers. Or sow seed in early March. Seed packets usually contain mixed colors.

G. uniflora. TRAILING GAZANIA. Trailing stems covered with

FRAGARIA CHILOENSIS
(Sand strawberry)

GAZANIA UNIFLORA
(Trailing gazania)

HEDERA HELIX (small-leafed form)
(English ivy)

HEDERA CANARIENSIS
(Algerian ivy)

HEDERA HELIX
(English ivy)

HELXINE SOLEIROLII
(Baby's tears)

HYPERICUM CALYCINUM
(Aaron's beard)

silvery gray foliage cover rapidly; grows 6 to 10 inches high. It bears yellow daisy flowers 2½ inches wide most of the year. Use on banks, level areas; will grow in poor soil. Plant 18 to 24 inches apart.

Feed all gazanias once a year with a slow acting fertilizer. Need little maintenance—an occasional deep watering about twice per month is usually sufficient. It's best to replant every three to four years. May have some trouble with weeds.

GERANIUM, ivy. See *Pelargonium peltatum*.

GINGER, wild. See *Asarum caudatum*.

GOUT WEED. See *Aegopodium podograria*.

HEATH. See *Erica carnea*.

HEATHER, Scotch. See *Calluna vulgaris*.

HEDERA. IVY. Two species of ivy are used with equal generosity as ground covers or as vines—the English and the Algerian. The latter is not as hardy as the English, and has only one variety. English ivy offers so many variations that it's next to impossible to classify them. Both cover the ground with long leafy runners that root at the joints, or they cling to walls, fences, etc. by aerial rootlets.

H. canariensis. ALGERIAN IVY. CANARY ISLAND IVY. Bright green leaves are 5 to 8 inches wide, 3 to 5 lobed, and more widely spaced along the stems than English ivy. It's also more tolerant of hot sun. Variety 'Variegata' has leaves edged with greenish white.

H. helix. ENGLISH IVY. Leaves dark green with paler veins. On sterile shoots are broadly ovate to triangular leaves, 3 to 5-lobed, 2 to 4 inches wide at base and as long. On fertile shoots leaves are not lobed and are more ovate. Variety 'Baltica' is hardier.

English ivy has a prodigious capacity for producing stems with leaves completely different from those on the rest of the plant. When cuttings are made of these stems, a new variety comes into existence. The many small and miniature-leafed forms are extremely useful for ground covers because of their more restrained growth habit, useful in smaller areas.

Some of the small leafed forms are: 'Hahns Self Branching'—light green leaves, dense branching; variety 'Conglomerata'—a slow-growing dwarf; variety 'Minima'—leaves ½ to 1 inch across with 3 to 5 angular lobes. An idea of the variety in forms can be had from a few of the names of the ivies in the trade: 'California Beauty,' 'Dragon Tongue,' 'Fan,' 'Gold Dust,' 'Maple Leaf,' 'Needle Point,' 'Pin Oak,' and many more.

Plant rooted cuttings 18 inches apart. To keep plantings looking tidy, trim severely every two or three years, especially the large leafed kinds. In fact, a yearly mowing will keep planting under control. Water deeply during hot summer months—especially Algerian ivy.

Ivy grows like some horses race—slow at the start but mighty fast in the home stretch. For a year or two the ivy sprigs 18 inches apart will look as though they will never fill in. Weeds will sprout continually in the open spaces. Keep up the feeding and watering. Suddenly very fast growth will begin.

HELIANTHEMUM NUMMULARIUM. SUN ROSE. Mostly prostrate evergreen shrublets with dense glossy green or gray-

DELOSPERMA 'ALBA'
(Ice plant)

JUNIPERUS CHINENSIS 'SAN JOSE'
(San Jose juniper)

green foliage, compact or somewhat trailing, and growing 6 to 8 inches high, with 3-foot spread. Many forms with gay flowers in pink, peach, apricot, orange, yellow, white, or red; single or double depending on the variety. Bloom profusely from April to June; again in fall if sheared back severely after first bloom. Each flower lasts a day, or half a day, but buds continue to open regularly over a long period of time.

Set container-grown plants 12 to 18 inches apart. Sun roses are somewhat slow to establish. Try not to disturb the roots. The plants tend to get woody when older; replace after 7 or 8 years.

HELXINE SOLEIROLII. BABY'S TEARS, ANGEL TEARS. Creeping, moss-like, little perennial herb with light green, tiny, round leaves, and inconspicuous white flowers. Lush and fragile-looking, it forms a dense mat 2 to 3 inches high.

Roots readily from any piece of stem. May become a pest. Get quicker coverage if planted from plugs or plant divisions. Some nurseries supply it in flats. Set plants 6 to 18 inches apart. Needs ample moisture. In hot climates, it is the best ground cover for shady places. Occasional trimming needed. Because of dense growth and shade, weeds are not too much of a problem—but occasionally some annual bluegrass shows up in it.

HONEYSUCKLE. See *Lonicera*

HYMENOCYCLUS. See Ice plant.

HYPERICUM CALYCINUM. AARON'S BEARD. Spreading evergreen, or semi-deciduous in cold areas, to 1 foot high. Leaves are cool medium green in sun, yellow-green in shade, 4 inches long. Brilliant splashes of bright yellow, 3-inch-wide flowers with showy masses of stamens appear in the heat of the summer.

Start from flats, or rooted stems dug out from established planting. Set 18 inches apart. Spreads by means of underground runners—strong and invasive in sun, but controlled in shade. Excellent soil binder for steep banks if watered. Cut plants back to ground every second or third year during dormant season. Weeds are no problem once it's established. In fact, this hypericum grows and spreads through garden beds worse than many weeds.

IBERIS SEMPERVIRENS. EVERGREEN CANDYTUFT. Low growing compact mounds to 8 to 12 inches, spreading to 2 feet. Excellent dark green foliage, fresh looking throughout the year. Flat clusters of small snowy white flowers from early spring until June.

Set container-grown plants 3 feet apart, or increase by cuttings. Shear back occasionally to keep it neat and encourage new bloom.

ICE PLANT. Usually sold in the nurseries under the name of mesembryanthemum. Actually the plants normally sold under this name are in several different genera—*Cryophytum, Carpobrotus, Lampranthus, Oscularia, Delosperma, Drosanthemum,* and *Hymenocyclus.* Ice plants are annual, or evergreen succulent-stemmed perennials with fleshy leaves on trailing or semi-erect stems. Daisy-like flowers in all colors except blue, so profuse in number and so intense in color, the effect is often blinding.

Plant cuttings of plants 12 to 18 inches apart or by the specia process shown on page 109. Also may be grown from seed; wil

JUNIPERUS HORIZONTALIS 'DOUGLASII'
(Waukegan juniper)

self-sow once they are planted. Will take moderate amount of moisture if soil is well drained. Perennials do not withstand severe frosts. Faded flowers are unsightly and should be removed. May need cutting back every 3 or 4 years to renew growth and increase flowering stems.

INSIDE-OUT FLOWER. See *Vancouveria planipetala.*

IRISH MOSS. See *Arenaria verna caespitosa.*

IVY. See *Hedera.*

JAPANESE SPURGE. See *Pachysandra terminalis.*

JEWEL MINT OF CORSICA. See *Mentha requienii.*

JUNIPERUS. JUNIPERS. The low-growing junipers probably rate at the top of the list for evergreen ground covers that maintain a height of about 2 feet, and they are attractive all year. They come in a wide selection of foliage color and form. Here are a few:

J. chinensis varieties: 'Pfitzeriana Compacta.' Grows to 2 feet high and 2 feet wide. Blue, lacy foliage. 'San Jose.' Grows to 2 feet high and 6 feet or more wide. Heavy trunked, dark sage green foliage. Slow growing. Variety *sargentii* spreads slowly to form a broad rounded mound. Light green foliage of fine texture.

J. communis saxatilis. DWARF JUNIPER. Grows to 1 foot high and 6 feet wide. A ground cover for small areas. Trailing branches with silvery upturned branchlets like tiny candles.

J. conferta. SHORE JUNIPER. A low, 1 to 2-foot-high, uneven, and informal mat of blue-green foliage. Leaves all needle-like. Stands salt spray and submergence. Not adapted to hot summer climates.

J. horizontalis. *(J. prostrata).* CREEPING JUNIPER. Prostrate, creeping to form a low, 18-inch-high, compact mat of blue-gray foliage. Variety 'Bar Harbor,' considered very choice by many, has gray-green foliage. Variety 'Douglasii,' Waukegan juniper, is moderately fast growing, spreading to 20 feet or more, and to less than 2 feet high. Soft metallic blue foliage turns interesting shades of purplish blue in fall. Variety 'Plumosa,' Andorra juniper, is spreading, slightly mounding to 15 to 18 inches, with gray-green feathery foliage tinged bronze in fall. Variety 'Wiltonii.' Flattest juniper, 4 to 6 inches high, 8 to 10 feet wide. Dense short branchlets on long trailing branches. Intense silver blue color.

J. procumbens 'Nana.' Grows to 1 foot high and 4 to 5 feet wide. A choice blue-gray juniper; extremely dense and slow. Mounds slightly but never shows trunk or branches.

J. sabina 'Tamariscifolia.' TAMARIX JUNIPER. Wide spreading to 15 feet or more, and frequently less than 18 inches high, with sprays of rather fine, bright green foliage.

J. scopulorum 'White Silver King.' Grows to 10 inches high and 10 feet wide. Extremely hardy and tolerant of heat and wind. Pale silvery blue foliage.

J. virginiana 'Silver Spreader.' Grows to 1½ feet high and 8 feet wide. Silvery green, lacy, fine textured foliage branches.

KINNIKINNICK. See *Arctostaphylos uva-ursi.*

KNOTWEED, rose carpet. See *Polygonum vaccinifolium.*

KOREAN GRASS. See *Zoysia tenuifolia.*

LAMB'S EARS. See *Stachys olympica.*

LAMPRANTHUS. See ice plant.

LANTANA MONTEVIDENSIS. *(L. sellowiana).* TRAILING LANTANA. A low, rapid grower wih trailing branches to 3 feet. Small, 1-inch leaves, and fragrant lavender-pink flowers in dense clusters.

Newer forms of trailing lantanas offer yellow, orange, or white flowers.

Start with rooted cuttings, plants in flats or plants in gallon containers. Set 18 inches apart. Cut back and thin yearly to keep

JUNIPERUS SABINA 'TAMARISCIFOLIA'
(Tamarix juniper)

LANTANA MONTEVIDENSIS
(Trailing lantana)

LOTUS BERTHELOTII
(Parrot's beak)

LONICERA JAPONICA 'HALLIANA'
(Halls Japanese honeysuckle)

plants from becoming woody and sparsely foliaged. Plants are best when not fertilized or overwatered. Full sun is an absolute essential.

LAVENDER COTTON. See *Santolina.*

LILY-OF-THE-VALLEY. See *Convallaria majalis.*

LILY TURF. See *Liriope.*

LINGONBERRY. See *Vaccinium vitis-idaea.*

LINNAEA BOREALIS. TWINFLOWER. Dainty, flat, ever-green mat of small, glossy, 1-inch-long leaves. Spreads by vining runners. Pale pink, twin, bell-like flowers ⅓ inch long on each 4-inch stem.

Start from container-grown plants. Set 3 to 6 inches apart. Requires adequate moisture. Mulch with leaf mold to keep it rooting. Weeds no problem if planted in weed-free woods duff and kept well mulched.

LIPPIA, garden. See *Phyla nodiflora.*

LIRIOPE. LILY TURF. Each plant is an evergreen fountain of dark green, narrow, grass-like leaves; forming shaggy mats. Small flowers in spikes may or may not overtop the foliage.

L. muscari. BIG BLUE LILY TURF. Leaves firm, ¾ inch wide, and 18 inches long. Dense clusters of small violet flowers are thick among the grass-like leaves, in summer.

L. spicata. CREEPING LILY TURF. Leaves narrower, about ¼-inch broad. Flower spike slender, flowers light lilac to almost white.

Start from divisions or container-grown plants. Set 12 inches apart.

LONICERA JAPONICA 'Halliana.' HALLS JAPANESE HONEYSUCKLE. Fast growing, wide covering vine that covers ground very well, especially on slopes. So vigorous it must be controlled with sharp shears or it will become a weed. Evergreen to semi-deciduous. Deep green, oval, 3-inch-long leaves. White flowers changing to yellow, in late spring and summer; fragrant.

Start from stem cuttings rooted in sand, or from well established flat-grown plants. Set 24 inches apart. Can also be grown from gallon-can-size plants; set 3 feet apart. These will give more rapid coverage but may give a more moundy effect. Weeds not too much of a problem but Bermuda grass may work through the sparse spots.

LOTUS. Here are two ground-cover lotus that are so different in habit, foliage, flower color, and garden function that they must be discussed separately.

L. berthelotii. Trailing evergreen shrub with slender 2 to 3-foot-long branches covered thickly with fine textured, silvery gray foliage, the whole effect being that of a soft, fluffy shawl. Narrow, sweet pea-shaped, 1-inch flowers, scarlet fading to orange. Blooms in June and July.

Start from rooted cuttings, flats, or established plants in pots or containers. Set plants 24 inches apart. Foliage gives best appearance during warmer seasons of the year. Cool weather causes some leaf drop and bareness. Should be trimmed back every year to encourage new growth and keep it neat. If left unpruned, plants become extremely woody. Eventual cover is usually thick enough to eliminate most weeds.

L. corniculatus. BIRD'S FOOT TREFOIL. Makes a roughish frilly mat of dark green lush foliage, studded in summer and fall with clusters of small yellow flowers. Seed pods so arranged on the top of the stalk that they look like a bird's foot.

Start from divisions set 6 inches apart For a rough country lawn, or a garden problem area it's best to sow seeds. In cold climate it's barren in winter, but semi-evergreen in mild climates. Needs water in the hot dry months. Also will take more water

MYOSOTIS SCORPIOIDES (foreground)
(True forget-me-not)

OPHIOPOGON JAPONICUS
(Mondo grass)

PACHYSANDRA TERMINALIS
(Japanese spurge)

than a lawn. When planted as a lawn should be mowed but only about half as often. Although you can call it a lawn it always resembles a neatly mowed field of alfalfa.

LYSIMACHIA NUMMULARIA. MONEYWORT, CREEPING JENNIE OR CHARLIE. Creeping evergreen perennial that sends out long runners to 2 feet long that root at the joints. Ultimately forms a pretty, light green, ruffly mat of roundish leaves. Flowers bright yellow, ⅔ to 1-inch wide, bloom in July and August. Start from divisions set 12-18 inches apart. Requires adequate moisture (accepts marshy conditions) and fairly dense shade.

MAHONIA REPENS. CREEPING MAHONIA. Bluish green leaves with 3 to 7 leaflets have spines on the edges like holly. The foliage grows rather densely on the 10-inch-high stems. In spring it forms small yellow flowers in 3-inch-long clusters at the ends of the branches. These flowers are followed by black grape-like fruits in summer. Plant 12 inches apart.

MENTHA REQUIENII. JEWEL MINT OF CORSICA. Miniature, moss-like, perennial creeper, growing only ½-inch high. Flat, compact, cushiony mat of delicate, tiny, round, brilliant green leaves. Diminutive, light purple or violet flowers in summer. When pinched, or crushed underfoot, it releases a refreshing fragrance somewhat like sage.
Start from divisions set 6 inches apart. Best green in early summer. In cold-weather areas may disappear in winter.

MESEMBRYANTHEMUM. See ice plant.

MOCK STRAWBERRY. See *Duchesnea indica*.

MONDO GRASS. See *Ophiopogon japonicus*.

MONEYWORT. See *Lysimachia nummularia*.

MORNING GLORY, ground. See *Convolvulus mauritanicus*.

MOSS PINK. See *Phlox subulata*.

MUEHLENBECKIA AXILLARIS (sometimes sold as *M. nana*). CREEPING WIRE VINE. An unusual little plant with small wiry stems that grow close to the ground and bear many small,

round, bronzy green leaves. Plants grow 2 to 4 feet high. Set them out 6 to 12 inches apart.

MYOSOTIS SCORPIOIDES. TRUE FORGET-ME-NOT. This plant is similar to the common forget-me-not, but it grows lower, flowers more continually, and its roots live over from year to year. From spring to fall it grows 6 to 18 inches high and has narrow 1 to 2-inch-long leaves. In late spring and early summer many, little ¼-inch-wide flowers form—blue with yellow, pink, or white centers. Sow seed or plant divisions.

MYRTLE. See *Vinca*.

NATAL PLUM. See *Carissa grandiflora*.

NEPETA. This genus includes two ground cover species that are quite dissimilar. The only definite resemblance between the two is the individual flower structure.

N. hederacea. GROUND IVY, GILL-OVER-THE-GROUND. In some areas this one has volunteered so widely that it is considered a weed. In other areas it's seldom seen except where planted, in which case it makes a rather pleasing informal cover good for sunny or shaded situations, and thriving with very little maintenance. It grows 3 to 6 inches high and spreads by means of long creeping stems that root at the joints. Bright green round leaves have coarsely scalloped edges. Light blue flowers among the leaves in spring and summer. Plant 12 inches apart.

N. mussinii. CATMINT. Known chiefly for its soft gray-green foliage in attractive undulating mats to 2 feet high. There is a fragrance to the leaves. Cats enjoy rolling in plantings of it to intoxicate themselves on the fragrance in the same way as they do in the closely related catnip *(N. cataria)*. Difficult to keep neat if many cats prowl your neighborhood. Lavender blue, ½-inch flowers in loose spikes make a colorful display in early summer. If dead flower spikes prove unsightly, shear them back. This may bring on a second blooming cycle. Set plants 12 to 18 inches apart.

OPHIOPOGON JAPONICUS. MONDO GRASS. Billowy carpet of dark green grass-like leaves. Light lavender flowers bloom in early summer on stems about 12 inches long; followed by tight clusters of blue berries.

Least expensive starts are with root divisions taken at any time of the year, but this method is a little slow. Get quicker cover by planting established plants grown in pots, or gallon cans; some available in flats. To get a soft floating effect, plant single divisions 6 inches apart; larger plants set farther apart will give a coarser effect.

A spring feeding will give more vigorous growth. Mow every 3 to 4 years. Best to do this in early spring because recovery is slow. Dead leaves from trees and shrubs rake out easily. Weeding is a problem the first season as plants cover rather slowly. Bermuda grass may be a problem in sunny locations.

NEW ZEALAND BRASS BUTTONS. See *Cotula squalida*.

OSCULARIA. See ice plant.

OSTEOSPERMUM FRUTICOSUM (*Dimorphotheca fruticosa*). TRAILING AFRICAN DAISY. This attractive spreading perennial is seen mostly in Southern California, where it was introduced as a ground cover in 1960. It has pinkish mauve, daisy-like flowers about 3 inches in diameter. The light green, fleshy leaves are distinctive, and the plants grow about 1½ feet high. Plant 2 feet apart.

PACHISTIMA CANBYI. CANBY PACHISTIMA, RAT-STRIPPER. This native of eastern United States is a very hardy, acid-loving, finely textured, evergreen foliage plant that lends itself to use as a ground cover and as a low clipped hedge, or edging plant. A Western species, *P. myrsinites* (mountain lover, Oregon boxwood) is quite similar but has slightly larger leaves (¾ inch long), and grows taller.

PACHYSANDRA TERMINALIS. JAPANESE SPURGE. Hardy perennial herb with clean, crisp, evergreen foliage. Rich, dark green, 2 to 4-inch-long leaves arranged in fan-like clusters. In heavy shade it grows 10 inches high, in dappled shade to 6 inches. Leaves turn yellow in full sun. Plants spread by means of underground runners. Small, fluffy spikes of fragrant white flowers in summer; followed by soft white berries.

Start from rooted cuttings or divisions planted 6 to 12 inches apart. Requires rich soil on acid side with plenty of moisture, particularly while getting established. Keep weeded until well established.

PEARLWORT, Corsican. See *Sagina subulata*.

PELARGONIUM PELTATUM. IVY GERANIUM. Trailing plants to 2 to 3 feet or longer. Smooth, glossy, bright green leaves to 2 to 3 inches broad, 5-lobed like ivy. Few to several, 1-inch-wide, single or double flowers in rounded clusters on long stems are white, pink, rose, red, and lavender, often blotched in contrasting colors. In coastal areas it blooms all year; inland, the bloom is best during warm periods; plants look shabby after first frosts.

If started with unrooted stem cuttings, put 3 or 4 in each hole; usually one will survive. For faster coverage plant rooted cuttings out of flats. Set about 15 inches apart.

Does not require too much feeding except to encourage new growth after a severe frost, or a long period of neglect. Cut back in spring after frosts to encourage new growth and more prolific bloom. Weeding is difficult because of heavy growth. In areas where ivy geranium grows faster (the Southwest), experienced gardeners expect to replant it every 3 to 5 years.

PERIWINKLE. See *Vinca*.

PHLOX SUBULATA. MOSS PINK, GROUND PINK. Creeping mat-forming perennial to 6 inches high, with crowded, ½-inch, stiff, needle-like leaves. The ¾-inch flowers range in color from pink, rose, and scarlet, to lavender-blue, and white. Bloom in late spring and early summer. There are number of horticultural varieties.

Set plants out 12 to 18 inches apart. Or sow seeds in spring—it will take longer. After flowering cut back halfway. Keep weeded until well established.

PHYLA NODIFLORA (*Lippia repens*). GARDEN LIPPIA. Creeping and spreading to form a flat, ground-hugging mat with pale green foliage. Lilac to rose flowers clustered in small, dense, cushiony, ½-inch heads in spring, summer, and fall.

Start plants from rooted stolons or plant divisions. From well rooted plants in flats, cut out 1 or 2-inch squares. Plant divisions or rooted stolons 12 inches apart. Plant well established flat sod around 2 feet apart.

Of all the ground covers listed here, this is one of the half dozen that can be walked on, just like a lawn.

An annual top dressing of rich soil, humus, or compost will bring it out of its winter brown, dead look. Feeding is also helpful. Mow it to make growth more even; and to keep flowers off plants which attract quantities of bees. Particularly good in desert areas in extreme sun and heat.

PINK. See *Dianthus*.

POINT REYES CEANOTHUS. See *C. gloriosus*.

POLYGONUM. Three attractive ground covers belong to this group which also includes woody vines, annuals, perennials, many bad weeds, and some floating water plants. Flowers are small but showy because of their abundance—and their color—pinks, rose, or white.

P. capitatum. Perennial with trailing branches to 10 inches long. Elliptic leaves are 1½ inches long. Dense heads of pink flowers are ¾ inches across. Reseeds itself.

P. cuspidatum compactum (*P. reynoutria*). Fast growing perennial to 18 inches in full sun, or 24 inches in partial shade. Spreads by underground runners to about 3 feet. Wiry stems are clothed with pale green, heart-shaped, red-veined leaves that turn a brilliant red in fall. Plants are herbaceous, dying completely to the ground in winter. Flowers are carried in dense, showy clusters. Red in bud, they open to pale pink, providing a delicate lacy pattern above stiff coarse foliage.

For *P. cuspidatum compactum*, use underground runners to start, or plant out of gallon containers. Set 2 feet apart. Feed once a year. Needs trimming around the edges. Becomes heavily infested with mealybug when planted too deep, or if old dead leaves are allowed to accumulate around the crown. Annual weeds may be a problem until foliage comes out in spring. To correct this, mulch heavily with a clean mulch material.

For *P. capitatum:* Start with plants from flats or container-grown plants set about 1 foot apart. Brush off dead leaves and flowers in early spring.

POTENTILLA VERNA. SPRING CINQUEFOIL. Dainty, bright green, tufted creeper 2 to 6 inches high; leaves fern-like, divided into 5 leaflets. Butter-yellow stemless flowers in spring and summer.

Start container plants set 6 to 12 inches apart. Browns in winter in cold areas. Needs plenty of moisture. Very few weeds after the cover closes tight.

PYRACANTHA 'Santa Cruz.' In California, this red berried variety of the familiar firethorn, grows low enough and branches enough from the base to be grown as a ground cover. It is used for this purpose considerably along California freeways. White flowers in March and April. A very similar plant offered in some areas is P. 'Walderi'. Space plants of either kind 2 feet apart.

ROCKCRESS. See *Arabis caucasica*.

ROSE. 'Mermaid' and Banksia (*Rosa banksiae*) roses are vigorous climbing types that cover ground well. 'Mermaid' has pale yellow, single flowers; Banksia flowers are white or yellow and fragrant. Memorial rose (*R. wichuraiana*) is a strong-growing, prostrate shrub that grows several feet each year and roots

PHLOX SUBULATA
(Moss pink)

POLYGONUM CAPITATUM
(Pink fleece-flower)

PELARGONIUM PELTATUM
(Ivy geranium)

Ground covers 99

along the stems as it grows. The plants grow about a foot high. White flowers come out in summer. Occasionally remove dead and useless canes and branches.

ROSMARINUS OFFICINALIS 'Prosratus'. DWARF ROSE-MARY. Low spreading form of the familiar culinary shrub. Spreads 4 to 8 feet wide and stays under 2 feet high. Dark green narrow leaves; light blue flowers in April and May. The variety 'Lockwood de Forest' has lighter bright foliage, bluer flowers.

Rooted cuttings grown in flats most economical. Plants in gallon containers will give fastest growth. Plant 24 inches apart.

If fed, foliage becomes greener, growth more vigorous, and plant does not become as woody. Thin out occasionally to encourage new growth. Drought resistant. When planted in dry areas, weeds are not as much of a problem.

SAGINA SUBULATA. CORSICAN PEARLWORT. Evergreen perennial that forms a mossy mat of light green ¼-inch leaves. Tiny flowers are white, in summer. Variety 'Aurea' has golden yellow foliage all year.

Start divisions from flat-grown plants; set 6 inches apart. Feed with weak liquid fish fertilizer. Keep weeded until established.

SANTOLINA CHAMAECYPARISSUS. LAVENDER COTTON. An evergreen, aromatic, compact plant which, if allowed to grow to its maximum height of 2 feet, becomes woody, uneven and ragged. Best treated as a clipped dwarf, and kept to 1 foot or less. Brittle, woody stems densely clothed with rough, finely divided, gray leaves. Best in spring when growth is new. Bright yellow, button-like, ¾-inch heads on unclipped plants in July and August. Shear flowers off after bloom or they will hang on and look brown and untidy.

Start with cuttings, or container-grown plants. Plant 3 feet apart. Frequent trimming necessary to keep neat. Ideal for desert gardens.

SARCOCOCCA HUMILIS. A broad-leafed evergreen grown chiefly for its narrow, waxy, dark green, oval shaped leaves set densely along the branches. You don't see the flowers but when

they're blooming in spring they give off an enjoyable sweet fragrance. Individual plants will grow 1½ feet high and spread as wide as 8 feet. It will grow in very shaded locations even where it gets no direct sun at all.

SASA PYGMAEA. DWARF BAMBOO. One of the smallest of all bamboos; very free running. Grows to 10 inches high. Foliage color best during spring to first frost period. Cold weather causes yellowing of some foliage and semi-dormant appearance.

Rooted side shoots taken in April and May from older plantings are the least expensive, but are slow to take hold. Plants in gallon containers are available and will cover the ground in shorter time. For quick cover, plant 12 inches apart, or if you are willing to wait—2 feet apart.

Feeding will speed coverage. When established, a regular mowing program will make this an ideal ground cover. No weeding problems because decaying leaves at base of plants will inhibit weed growth. Confine plantings by curbs or walls or it will creep into parts of the garden where it's not wanted. Its creeping, spreading habit is so pronounced that some plantsmen look upon dwarf bamboo as strictly a plant for soil conservation use.

SATUREJA DOUGLASII *(Micromeria chamissonis).* YERBA BUENA. Creeping perennial with minty, fragrant foliage. Small round or oval leaves, and small, white, lavender-tinted flowers. Plants spread as much as 3 feet across by means of long slender stems, rooting as they go. Re-root at the tips.

Start from rooted cuttings set 2 feet apart. Or sow seeds. Requires plenty of moisture and leaf mold, ground bark, or peat moss so that it can root easily and thus spread more rapidly. Must be weeded until well established.

SAXIFRAGA SARMENTOSA. STRAWBERRY GERANIUM. Trailing to 2 feet with runners rooting at joints. Round 4-inch leaves, like geraniums, are reddish below, veined with white above. Small, white, 1-inch-wide flowers.

Start from divisions or cuttings set 8 or 9 inches apart. If started from gallon cans, plant 18 inches apart. Requires plenty of moisture, looks sparse and spotty if allowed to stay dry.

SEDUM. STONECROP. Most sedums are all succulent, evergreen, low-growing plants with a trailing habit of growth. Some kinds have round leaves, some have flat leaves, but the leaves on all are thick and juicy on the inside. Some kinds are gray-green, some reddish-green. Sedum will grow in poor soil, sun or shade, and can get along with little moisture. However, to grow a bed of sedum you'll be proud of, give it a well-prepared soil, not too much shade, and water it regularly. Sedum has been a disappointment to many when planted in large areas. Some spots get too crowded, die out, and leave the planting looking something like a mangy dog.

In California, nurseries offer about 13 kinds of sedum. You should look at the different kinds in flats and make your selection on the basis of leaf size, total texture, height, flower color, and habit.

SILVER MOUND. See *Artemisia schmidtiana.*

SNOW-IN-SUMMER. See *Cerastium tomentosum.*

STACHYS OLYMPICA (often sold as *S. lanata*) LAMB'S EARS. Herbaceous perennial, with soft woolly gray leaves, growing to 18 inches and spreading twice as wide. Small purple flowers in spikes appear in summer.

Start with divisions or nursery-grown transplants in flats; set 18 inches apart. Winter appearance is very poor—leaves become mushy, frost kills much of the foliage. Spring feeding aids in restoring appearance. Trim back, clean out dead foliage, and cut back all tall stalks to the ground after winter rains and frosts are over. In a few weeks new growth appears. Water not more than once a month. Cover is usually thick enough to combat weeds.

STAR JASMINE. See *Trachelospermum jasminoides.*

STONECROP. See *Sedum.*

ROSMARINUS OFFICINALIS 'PROSTRATUS'
(Dwarf rosemary)

MIXTURE: SEDUM, ICE PLANT, BACCHARIS, OTHERS

STRAWBERRY. See *Fragaria.*
STRAWBERRY GERANIUM. See *Saxifraga sarmentosa.*
SUN ROSE. See *Helianthemum nummularium.*
SWEET FERN. See *Comptonia peregrina.*
SWEET WOODRUFF. See *Asperula odorata.*

TEUCRIUM CHAMAEDRYS. Dark green toothed leaves grow thickly on this low (1 foot) plant. In summer rose or red-purple, ¾-inch flowers form in loose spikes. As a ground cover it fills in best when sheared back once or twice a year to force more side branching. Space plants 2 feet apart.

THYMUS SERPYLLUM. MOTHER-OF-THYME, CREEPING THYME. Prostrate perennial forming flat-growing, close-napped carpet of tiny, dark green, aromatic leaves, soft and fragrant under foot. Small purplish white flowers bloom from June to September. T. *lanuginosus,* woolly thyme, has downy, silver gray leaves in flat to undulating mat 2 to 3 inches high. Seldom blooms.

Set divisions or plants from flats 6 to 12 inches apart in fall or spring. Withstands neglect, drought. Woolly thyme tends to look a bit ragged in winter, but never dies back completely.

TIARELLA CORDIFOLIA. ALLEGHENY FOAM FLOWER. A native of eastern United States, this perennial spreads rapidly and makes a ground cover that is attractive all year. Slightly heart-shaped leaves are green mottled with brown, and they turn red bronze in autumn. In May, small white flowers in fluffy clusters rise to 12 inches above the foliage. Space plants 12 inches apart.

TRACHELOSPERMUM JASMINOIDES. STAR JASMINE. A vine that can be trained as a ground cover. Leaves are sturdy, lustrous, dark green. Clusters of very fragrant, small, white flowers in June and July. Makes a dense foliaged, luxurious ground cover.

Start from plants in gallon containers or small pots. Plant 1½ to 3 feet apart depending on how fast you want it to cover the ground completely. To encourage new growth, feed at least twice a year, in spring and late summer. To encourage this plant to grow as a ground cover with strong side branches, cut back the upright shoots and tack down the side branches with heavy wires bent like hairpins. Spray for scale during fall. Several seasons of weeding required. Grows thick enough after third or fourth year.

TWINFLOWER. See *Linnaea borealis.*

VACCINIUM VITIS-IDAEA. LINGONBERRY. Evergreen shrublet, slowly growing to 1 foot high, increasing and spreading by runners to 3 feet. Leaves are dark green, lustrous above, paler beneath; nodding bell-shaped flowers, white or pink, appearing in May, followed by edible red berries. Variety *minus,* mountain

THYMUS LANUGINOSUS
(Woolly thyme)

TIARELLA CORDIFOLIA
(Allegheny foam flower)

cranberry, is even more dwarfed than the species. Leaves smaller, and the flowers rose-pink or reddish.

Start container-grown plants set 9 inches apart. Requires lots of moisture. Mulch with peat moss or leaf mold. Unless ground is treated to kill weeds and grass there will be competition until the lingonberry is well established.

VANCOUVERIA PLANIPETALA *(V. parviflora).* INSIDE-OUT FLOWER. This is a delicate woods plant (a close relative of the barberries and epimediums) with much divided, dark green leaves, and an affinity for moisture and shade. It grows to 1½ feet high and forms small, white flowers in feathery clusters in May and June. In cold-winter climates the plants die to the ground each winter. Space plants 12 inches apart.

VERBENA PERUVIANA. Perennial but grown as an annual in cold areas. Creeping stems form prostrate mats. Rather hairy grayish foliage. Flowers rich scarlet in head-like clusters. Blooms are at their best during warm seasons; along coast there may be some bloom the year around.

Grows readily from rooted stolons, cuttings rooted in sand. Plant 18 inches apart. Foliage is good along the coast almost year around, but inland early frosts slow it down and the foliage seems to shrink. Growth is not thick enough to keep all weeds out, so for several seasons it will probably be necessary to weed. Watch for red spider mites. Replanting may be necessary every 2 to 3 years as stems grow away from the root crown.

VERONICA REPENS. CREEPING SPEEDWELL. Fine-textured, mat-forming plant that makes a low (4-inch) neat ground cover of uniform appearance, with lustrous green, oval-shaped, ½-inch leaves. Small rose or bluish white flowers in clusters form in late spring. Space plants 6 to 12 inches apart.

VINCA. PERIWINKLE, MYRTLE. Trailing or creeping evergreens.

V. major. COMMON PERIWINKLE. Glossy, dark green, 2-inch, oval leaves. Lavender-blue 1-inch-wide flowers on a trailing plant that may grow to 2 feet high. Generally 6 to 12 inches high where it has room to spread. May spread as much as 10 to 15 feet.

V. minor. DWARF PERIWINKLE. To 6 inches high, spreading to 10 feet. Like *V. major* but more dwarf, with smaller leaves and flowers. Blooms freely in early spring and again in fall. Has tendency to mound but becomes more compact when clipped annually. There are forms with white, wine red, and deeper blue flowers.

Start with rooted divisions (from flats). Set 18 inches *(V. minor)* to 24 inches *(V. major)* apart.

V. major: Requires lots of water in sun. Cutting back every four or five years will renew growth and provide thicker cover. Ultimately grows thick enough to keep out weeds.

V. minor: Best foliage color is in light shade, if fed several times a year in spring and fall, and given two to three good

TRACHELOSPERMUM JASMINOIDES
(Star jasmine)

ZOYSIA TENUIFOLIA
(Korean grass)

soakings per month. Some gardeners prefer to cut back in alternate years, others prefer to cut as close to ground as possible—not later than September to produce new growth before cold weather. Feed and water well after cutting. Clipping keeps growth more even. Very little competition from weeds.

WALL ROCKCRESS. See *Arabis caucasica.*

WINTER CREEPER. See *Euonymus fortunei.*

WINTERGREEN. See *Gaultheria procumbens.*

WIRE VINE, creeping. See *Muehlenbeckia axillaris.*

XANTHORHIZA SIMPLICISSIMA. YELLOW ROOT. Woodsy plant that thrives in moist soils in sun or shade. Green leaves made up of 5 leaflets, often lobed and divided, turn orange in the fall before they drop. The stems grow to a uniform height making a rather even surface, usually about 2 feet high. It increases rapidly by suckers and spreading roots. Space rooted cuttings 2 feet apart.

YARROW, woolly. See *Achillea tomentosa.*

YELLOW ROOT. See *Xanthorhiza simplicissima.*

YERBA BUENA. See *Satureja douglasii.*

ZOYSIA TENUIFOLIA. KOREAN GRASS. A creeping, fine-textured grass that makes a beautiful living tapestry. It's hardy but turns brown in cold weather. It needs water, takes sun or shade. Humps are havens for slugs, insects. Plant pieces from flats 8 inches apart.

VINCA MINOR
(Dwarf periwinkle)

Ground cover summary

Below and on the following pages, we have charted the vital statistics for the ground covers listed on pages 82 through 103. In column 3 of the chart, "rapid" covering of the ground means complete coverage within a year under most conditions. A "slow" ground cover usually takes 2 years or longer. Plants marked X in the "Steep slopes" column grow satisfactorily in such situations without falling down, causing landslides, or failing because of skimpy watering. Some ground covers do a fine job on large areas but look coarse in small plots. Others develop bare spots in large areas. These differences are indicated in columns 5 and 6 of the chart.

	Hardy to	Where common: entire country (US); east, mid-west, and Rockies (E); California-Arizona (CA); Pacific Northwest (NW)	How fast to cover ground	Steep slopes (over 25 %)	Large areas (over 500 sq. ft.)	Small areas (under 500 sq. ft.)	Full sun	Sun to medium shade	Medium shade to full shade	Tolerates dry or poor soil	Tolerates acid, moist soil
Achillea tomentosa	Sub-zero	US	Rapid			X	X	X		X	
Aegopodium podograria	Sub-zero	E	Rapid	X	X	X	X	X	X	X	X
Ajuga reptans	3°	US	Rapid	X	X	X	X	X			
Andromeda polifolia	Sub-zero	E	Slow			X	X	X			X
Anthemis nobilis	0°	US	Mod.	X	X	X	X	X		X	
Arabis caucasica	Sub-zero	US	Mod.			X	X			X	
Arctostaphylos uva-ursi	Sub-zero	US	Slow	X	X	X	X	X		X	X
Arenaria balearica	5°	E	Rapid			X	X	X			X
A. verna caespitosa	Sub-zero	E	Mod. to rapid			X	X	X			X
Armeria maritima	Sub-zero	US	Mod. to rapid			X	X			X	
Artemisia schmidtiana	Sub-zero	E	Rapid	X		X	X			X	
Asarum caudatum	Sub-zero	US	Mod.		X	X			X		X
Asparagus sprengeri	25°	CA	Slow to Mod.	X	X	X	X	X		X	
Asperula odorata	Sub-zero	US	Rapid			X			X		X
Baccharis pilularis	3°	CA	Rapid	X	X		X	X		X	
Bergenia crassifolia	15°	US	Mod.		X	X		X	X		X
Bougainvillea	28°	CA	Rapid	X	X		X				
Calluna vulgaris	Sub-zero	US	Slow to Mod.	X	X	X	X	X		X	X
Campanula carpatica	Sub-zero	US	Mod.			X	X	X			X
C. elatines garganica	Sub-zero	US	Mod.			X		X			X
C. portenschlagiana	Sub-zero	US	Slow to mod.			X		X	X		X
C. poscharskyana	Sub-zero	US	Mod.	X		X		X			X

	Hardy to	Where common: entire country (US); east, mid-west, and Rockies (E); California-Arizona (CA); Pacific Northwest (NW)	How fast to cover ground	Steep slopes (over 25%)	Large areas (over 500 sq. ft.)	Small areas (under 500 sq. ft.)	Full sun	Sun to medium shade	Medium shade to full shade	Tolerates dry or poor soil	Tolerates acid, moist soil
Carissa grandiflora	25 to 28°	CA	Slow to mod.		X	X	X	X			
Ceanothus gloriosus	10°	CA	Mod. to rapid	X	X		X			X	
C. griseus horizontalis	10°	CA	Mod. to rapid	X	X		X			X	
C. thyrsiflorus repens	10°	CA	Mod. to rapid	X	X	X	X	X			
Cerastium tomentosum	Sub-zero	US	Rapid	X	X	X	X	X		X	
Ceratostigma plumbaginoides	Sub-zero	US	Mod. to rapid	X	X	X	X	X		X	
Comptonia peregrina	Sub-zero	E	Rapid	X	X		X			X	X
Convallaria majalis	Sub-zero	E, NW	Rapid			X			X	X	X
Convolvulus mauritanicus	0°	CA	Mod. to rapid			X	X			X	
Cornus canadensis	Sub-zero	E, NW	Slow to mod.			X	X	X			X
Coronilla varia	Sub-zero	E	Rapid	X	X		X	X		X	
Cotoneaster adpressa	Sub-zero	US	Slow to mod.	X	X	X	X	X		X	
C. dammeri	Sub-zero	US	Slow to mod.	X	X	X	X	X		X	
C. horizontalis	Sub-zero	US	Mod.	X	X	X	X	X		X	
C. microphylla	5°	US	Mod.	X	X	X	X	X		X	
Cotula squalida	0°	US	Rapid		X	X	X	X		X	
Dianthus	Sub-zero	US	Mod.			X	X			X	
Duchesnea indica	Sub-zero	US	Rapid		X		X	X	X		X
Epimedium	Sub-zero	US	Mod.			X			X		X
Erica carnea	Sub-zero	US	Mod.	X	X	X	X	X			X
E. ciliaris	Sub-zero	US	Mod.	X		X	X	X			X
Erigeron karvinskianus	20°	CA	Rapid			X	X			X	
Erodium chamaedryoides	15°	CA	Mod.			X	X	X			
Euonymus fortunei	Sub-zero	US	Slow to mod.	X	X	X	X	X	X		X

	Hardy to	Where common: entire country (US); east, mid-west, and Rockies (E); California–Arizona (CA); Pacific Northwest (NW)	How fast to cover ground	Steep slopes (over 25%)	Large areas (over 500 sq. ft.)	Small areas (under 500 sq. ft.)	Full sun	Sun to medium shade	Medium shade to full shade	Tolerates dry or poor soil	Tolerates acid, moist soil
E.f. 'Colorata'	Sub-zero	US	Slow to mod.		X	X	X	X	X		X
E.f. 'Gracilis', Kewensis; and 'Minima'	Sub-zero	US	Slow to mod.			X	X	X	X		X
E.f. radicans	Sub-zero	US	Mod.	X	X	X	X	X	X		X
E.f. 'Vegeta'	Sub-zero	US	Slow to mod.	X	X	X	X	X	X		X
Festuca ovina 'Glauca'	5°	CA, NW	Rapid	X	X	X	X	X		X	
Fragaria chiloensis	0°	CA, NW	Rapid	X	X	X	X	X			X
Galax aphylla	Sub-zero	E, NW	Mod.			X			X		X
Gaultheria procumbens	Sub-zero	E, NW	Slow			X			X		X
Gaylussacia brachycera	Sub-zero	E	Slow		X			X	X		X
Gazania	10°	CA	Rapid	X	X	X	X			X	
Hedera canariensis	25°	CA	Rapid	X	X		X	X			
H. helix	Sub-zero	US	Rapid	X	X		X	X	X		X
H. helix (small-leafed forms)	Sub-zero	US	Rapid	X	X	X	X	X	X		X
Helianthemum nummularium	Sub-zero	US	Slow at first			X	X			X	
Helxine soleirolii	25°	CA	Rapid			X			X		X
Hypericum calycinum	0°	US	Rapid	X	X		X	X		X	
Iberis sempervirens	Sub-zero	US	Slow			X	X	X			
Ice plant	15 to 25°	CA	Rapid	X	X	X	X			X	
Juniperus chinensis 'Pfitzeriana Compacta'	Sub-zero	US	Mod.	X	X		X			X	
J.c. 'San Jose'	Sub-zero	US	Slow	X	X	X	X			X	
J.c. sargentii	Sub-zero	US	Mod.	X	X	X	X			X	
J. communis saxatilis	Sub-zero	US	Slow	X	X	X	X			X	
J. conferta	Sub-zero	US	Mod.	X	X	X	X	X			X
J. horizontalis and varieties	Sub-zero	US	Mod.	X	X	X	X			X	
J. procumbens 'Nana'	Sub-zero	US	Slow	X		X	X	X		X	
J. sabina 'Tamariscifolia'	Sub-zero	US	Mod.	X	X	X	X	X		X	
J. scopulorum 'White Silver King'	Sub-zero	US	Mod.	X	X	X	X			X	

	Hardy to	Where common: entire country (US); east, mid-west, and Rockies (E); California-Arizona (CA); Pacific Northwest (NW)	How fast to cover ground	Steep slopes (over 25%)	Large areas (over 500 sq. ft.)	Small areas (under 500 sq. ft.)	Full sun	Sun to medium shade	Medium shade to full shade	Tolerates dry or poor soil	Tolerates acid, moist soil
J. virginiana 'Silver Spreader'	Sub-zero	US	Mod.	X	X	X	X			X	X
Lantana montevidensis	30°	CA	Rapid	X	X		X			X	
Linnaea borealis	Sub-zero	E, NW	Mod.			X			X		X
Liriope muscari	Sub-zero	US	Mod.			X			X		
L. spicata	Sub-zero	US	Mod.			X			X		
Lonicera japonica 'Halliana'	Sub-zero	US	Rapid	X	X		X	X		X	X
Lotus berthelotii	30°	CA	Rapid	X	X	X	X	X			
L. corniculatus	10°	CA, NW	Rapid	X	X		X	X		X	
Lysimachia nummularia	Sub-zero	US	Rapid		X				X		X
Mahonia repens	Sub-zero	US	Slow to mod.	X	X	X		X	X		X
Mentha requienii	5°	US	Mod. to rapid		X		X	X	X		X
Muehlenbeckia axillaris	15°	CA	Mod.		X	X	X			X	
Myosotis scorpioides	Sub-zero	US	Rapid		X			X	X		X
Nepeta hederacea	Sub-zero	US	Rapid		X		X	X	X		X
N. mussinii	Sub-zero	US	Mod.		X	X	X			X	
Ophiopogon japonicus	0°	US	Slow to start		X	X	X	X	X		X
Osteospermum fruticosum	25°	CA	Mod.	X	X		X			X	
Pachistima canbyi	Sub-zero	E, NW	Slow to mod.		X	X	X	X			X
Pachysandra terminalis	Sub-zero	US	Rapid		X	X			X		X
Pelargonium peltatum	10 to 28°	CA	Rapid	X	X		X	X			
Phlox subulata	Sub-zero	US	Rapid	X	X	X	X	X			X
Phyla nodiflora	0°	CA, NW	Rapid	X	X		X			X	
Polygonum capitatum	20°	CA	Mod. to rapid			X	X	X			X
P. cuspidatum compactum	0°	US	Rapid	X	X		X			X	
Potentilla verna	0°	US	Mod.			X		X			X
Pyracantha	3°	CA, NW	Rapid	X	X		X	X		X	

	Hardy to	Where common: entire country (US); east, mid-west, and Rockies (E); California-Arizona (CA); Pacific Northwest (NW)	How fast to cover ground	Steep slopes (over 25%)	Large areas (over 500 sq. ft.)	Small areas (under 500 sq. ft.)	Full sun	Sun to medium shade	Medium shade to full shade	Tolerates dry or poor soil	Tolerates acid, moist soil
Roses — Banksia	20°	CA	Rapid	X	X		X				
Roses — 'Mermaid'	0°	US	Rapid	X	X		X				
Roses — Rosa wichuraiana	Sub-zero	E	Rapid	X	X		X	X			
Rosmarinus officinalis 'Lockwood de Forest'	3°	CA, NW	Slow at first	X	X	X	X			X	
R.o 'Prostratus'	3°	CA, NW	Slow at first	X	X	X	X	X		X	
Sagina subulata	Sub-zero	US	Rapid			X		X			X
Santolina chamaecyparissus	0°	US	Rapid	X	X	X	X			X	
Sarcococca humilis	Sub-zero	US	Slow			X			X		X
Sasa pygmaea	Sub-zero	US	Mod. to rapid			X	X	X			
Satureja douglasii	0°	CA, NW	Mod. to rapid			X		X	X	X	X
Saxifraga sarmentosa	0°	US	Rapid			X		X			X
Sedum	0 to 15°	US	Rapid	X	X	X	X	X		X	
Stachys olympica	Sub-zero	US	Rapid			X	X				
Teucrium chamaedrys	Sub-zero	US	Slow		X	X	X			X	
Thymus lanuginosus	Sub-zero	US	Rapid		X	X	X	X		X	
T. serpyllum	Sub-zero	US	Rapid		X	X	X	X		X	
Tiarella cordifolia	Sub-zero	E, NW	Slow			X			X		X
Trachelospermum jasminoides	10 to 25°	CA	Slow to start	X	X	X	X	X		X	X
Vaccinium vitis-idaea	Sub-zero	US	Slow			X		X	X		X
Vancouveria planipetala	Sub-zero	CA, NW	Mod.		X	X		X	X		X
Verbena peruviana	20°	CA	Rapid		X	X	X	X		X	
Veronica repens	Sub-zero	US	Rapid			X	X	X			X
Vinca major	0°	CA, NW	Rapid	X	X			X	X		X
Vinca minor	Sub-zero	US	Rapid	X	X	X		X	X		X
Xanthorhiza simplicissima	Sub-zero	E	Rapid	X	X		X	X	X		X
Zoysia tenuifolia	10°	CA	Mod. to rapid	X	X	X	X	X		X	

HOW TO PLANT GROUND COVERS

If you are going to plant a permanent ground cover, if you live in an arid climate, and if the plant is not described in the encyclopedia section as drought-resistant, the planting will need regular watering. You should install a sprinkler system. Install it as outlined for lawn sprinkler systems on page 32 to 41, before preparing the soil and planting. The heads will have to be on risers that extend above the ground surface.

Usually, it's wise to prepare the soil as thoroughly as you would for a lawn — up to but usually not including the lawn-building steps of levelling and rolling (necessary for only the lowest, most soil-hugging ground covers). Soil preparation instructions are given on pages 15 to 18. Thorough preparation with generous use of organic matter in the soil and inclusion of a phosphate fertilizer is especially important with fill land or soil from which topsoil has been removed. This kind of ground is usually composed of impoverished subsoil, rock, or shale. Iron sulfate or iron chelates are frequently needed on such soils to prevent leaves from turning yellow.

In the encyclopedia, several planting methods are mentioned repeatedly. Here, briefly, is what each term means. For more detailed instructions, see the planting chapter of the *Sunset* Book, *Basic Gardening Illustrated.*

Gallon cans. In Western United States, most small shrubs and large perennials are sold in gallon cans. The cans are now coming into popular use in the East. An 8-inch clay pot is about the same size.

Divisions. You dig up a root clump, divide it into segments, and plant the segments, known as divisions. Different plants divide in different ways.

BANK OF IVY being planted. Soil conditioner was mixed into soil, soil was pre-moistened, plants in flats were soaked before planting. Spacing for ivy: 18 inches

Cuttings. You remove a stem and insert its cut end several inches into the prepared soil, firm the soil around it, and water well. Roots will grow from the stems.

Rooted cuttings. These are stem sections taken as described for cuttings, but rooted in sand or similar material before being planted.

Stem segments. These are the diced-up sections of runners or shoots, as illustrated and described below.

Flats. These are long, low wooden boxes or trays in which nurseries grow small plants. You cut or tear the roots of each plant apart from its neighbors in the flat.

A WAY to get start for easy-rooting ground cover such as ice plant (warm climate item): cut long shoots from an existing planting while trimming it around the edges

CHOP shoots into small segments. Scatter segments on prepared soil like seed. Cover lightly with soil, keep it moist. On banks, make notches to hold the segments

Index

PHOTOGRAPHERS

William Aplin: 78, 84 (left), 86, 90 (right), 91 (top), 93 (right), 95, 96 (right), 99 (bottom right), 100, 101, 103 (top right), 109 (bottom). **Aplin-Dudley Studios:** 81. **Morley Baer:** 79. **Ernest Braun:** 84 (right), 103 (left). **Tom Burns Jr.:** 85 (left). **Carroll C. Calkins:** 90 (left). **Clyde Childress:** 28, 31 (bottom), 43, 44, 45, 47, 48, 51 (center, right), 52 (center, right), 53 (top left, bottom left), 62, 63, 64 (top left), 72 (top left), 73. **Glenn M. Christiansen:** 9, 102 (left). **Robert Cox:** 52 (left), 53 (top center), 64 (bottom). **Richard Dawson:** 30, 31 (top), 45 (right), 63 (top right), 64 (top right), 80 (top), 92 (left), 99 (bottom left). **Eastman Chemical Products, Inc.:** 38 (bottom). **Ferry-Morse Seed Company:** 2, 6. **Gottscho-Schleisner, Inc.:** 96 (left), 102 (right). **Jeannette Grossman:** 88, 89. **Robert Hamill:** 80 (bottom). **Art Hupy:** 103 (bottom). **Russell Illig:** 39 (bottom). **Kassler Studios:** 10, 77, 53 (top right, bottom right). **Roy Krell:** 92 (right). **Martin Litton:** 91 (bottom right). **Michael McGinnis:** 91 (bottom left). **Don Normark:** 85 (top right), 87 (top right), 99 (top). **Oregon State College:** 51 (left). **Marion Patterson:** 18 (top right, bottom right). **Kenneth R. Reeves:** 38 (top), 39 (top). **John Robinson:** 97. **O. M. Scott & Sons Co.:** Cover, 66. **Blair Stapp:** 20 (top right, bottom right), 72 (bottom). **Darrow M. Watt:** 15, 17, 18 (left), 19, 20, (top left, bottom left), 22, 26, 27, 72 (right), 83, 94. **Joseph F. Williamson:** 93 (top left), 109 (top). **Herman J. Willis:** 67.